W9-AXK-464

ALSO BY TOM SEGEV

One Palestine, Complete:
Jews and Arabs Under the British Mandate

The Seventh Million:
The Israelis and the Holocaust

1949: The First Israelis

Soldiers of Evil

ELVIS IN JERUSALEM

ELVIS
··· IN ···
JERUSALEM

Post-Zionism and the Americanization of Israel

TOM SEGEV

TRANSLATED BY HAIM WATZMAN

METROPOLITAN BOOKS

Henry Holt and Company · New York

Metropolitan Books
Henry Holt and Company, LLC
Publishers since 1866
115 West 18th Street
New York, New York 10011

Metropolitan Books™ is a registered trademark of
Henry Holt and Company, LLC.

Copyright © 2001 by Tom Segev
Translation Copyright © 2002 by Metropolitan Books
All rights reserved.

Published in Canada by Fitzhenry & Whiteside Ltd.,
195 Allstate Parkway, Markham, Ontario L3R 4T8.

Originally published in Israel as *Hatzionim Hahadashim*
by Keter Publishers, Jerusalem, in 2001

Library of Congress Cataloging-in-Publication Data

Segev, Tom, 1945–
 [Tsiyonim ha-hadasbim. English]
 Elvis in Jerusalem : post-Zionism and the Americanization of Israel / by
Tom Segev.
   p. cm.
 Includes index.
 ISBN 0-8050-7020-6 (hbk.)
 1. Zionism—Israel—History—20th century. 2. Post-Zionism. 3. Israel—
Civilization. 4. National characteristics, Israeli. I. Title.
DS149.5.I75 S4413 2002
956.94—dc21   2002020509

Henry Holt books are available for special promotions and
premiums. For details contact: Director, Special Markets.

First American Edition 2002

Designed by Kelly S. Too

Printed in the United States of America
1 3 5 7 9 10 8 6 4 2

ELVIS IN JERUSALEM

Introduction

One day when I was a student at the Hebrew University High School in Jerusalem, our literature teacher stormed into the room, beside himself. The teacher, A. B. Yehoshua, now a leading Israeli novelist, would often share his most deeply felt thoughts with us, and an experience he'd had the previous evening had roiled him badly. While walking down Hakeren Hakayemet Street in the Rehavia neighborhood, not far from the Hebrew Gymnasium, another high school, he had noticed a group of teenagers having a loud discussion under a streetlight. He was elated—he loved impassioned young people. But when he came closer and heard what they were talking about, he was terribly disappointed. They weren't debating Zionist values. The subject being discussed so fiercely was the cost of a Volkswagen Beetle in Germany.

Rehavia was a solid middle-class neighborhood, home to intellectuals and teachers who had fled Germany and Eastern Europe before and during World War II. This was the beginning of the 1960s and many of the families living there had begun receiving reparation payments from Germany. At about the same time, the first Beetles had made their appearance on Israel's roads. Zionism's visionaries, who liked to say that Israel would achieve normalcy the day it produced the first Jewish thief, would have been proud of those Rehavia kids. They were, after all, a first glimmer of normalcy. But good old Buli— Yehoshua's nickname—was appalled. Years later, I can still see him tugging at his wild hair in genuine despair: Such vapidity! Who cares about the cost of a car? And in Germany? In Germany, of all places!

At the time some of my classmates were devotees of a tiny cult they reverently referred to as "the movement." The movement in question was the Hatnu'a HaMe'uhedet, one of the many youth organizations sponsored by Israeli labor Zionism. Its members wore blue shirts that closed with red laces instead of buttons, and they told one another that when the day came they would renounce their degenerate urban lives and join the more just society of a kibbutz. They could identify with Yehoshua's revulsion—some of them are living on kibbutzim to this day. Many other students, myself among them, couldn't understand what on earth our teacher wanted from us.

My father, a Communist who came to Palestine as a refugee from Nazi Germany, was killed in Israel's War of Independence. Each year, on the memorial day commemorating soldiers who died, my mother received a letter from the defense minister. Each year, as the day approached, the minister would write to families of the fallen, assuring them that all our wars had been forced on us, that the sacrifice had not been in vain, that Israel was doing everything possible to make peace.

When I was a child it was the stamp that impressed me most—the minister's letter always came in a first-day cover. The next thing I looked for was the autograph. It took a while before I learned, to my deepest disappointment, that the minister's blue signature was actually machine-printed. I didn't like the minister's letters—I'm not sure why. Perhaps I saw them as outside interference in something that was very personal, almost intimate. The annual Memorial Day ceremonies at school also felt like an invasion of privacy. What right did they have to talk about me? I thought. I know, of course, that many people take comfort in society's participation in their personal sorrow—the national mourning, ceremonies, and melancholy songs on the radio. My generation grew up on the values of self-sacrifice, part of the heroic story of how Israel won its independence in 1948. I suppose there are also people who find solace in the annual letter from the minister of defense.

As the years went by, I began to pay attention to what the minister actually wrote in his letter. On the whole, what he wrote made me furious. When, much later, I reread the dozens of letters we had kept, all I found were the stock phrases of the national consensus. It is hard to see any real difference between Minister of Defense David Ben-Gurion's letters and Minister of Defense Menachem Begin's. Or between Levi Eshkol's and Ariel Sharon's. I was furious because in those letters I wanted the whole truth and nothing but the truth, and I didn't find it. Not all of Israel's wars had been forced on it; Israel had not always done all it could to prevent war; people had been killed for no reason at all.

Prime and Defense Minister Yitzhak Rabin sent us a letter with a very personal tone. "It is after twelve, very late at night, and this is the eighth or ninth time I have written to you. . . . And what can I write? It is already night and I know that you are tossing on your beds and sleep eludes you . . . your thoughts stray to the words and pictures and memories of your son, your daughter, your father, your husband, your brother. . . . They come back to you in your dreams, always young, teenagers who had only just begun to live, who wanted to live, to love, to build homes; young people who looked to the future with great hope that was cut down."

I'd have preferred the rough style of the Rabin I knew to this personal composition, because at that moment of truth what I wanted was the whole truth. "In my Memorial Day letters I have always written to you about peace," Rabin wrote. "It has come. It is hard, it is agonizing, it is battered, it keeps running up against obstacles. But it is here." That was in 1994. Peace wasn't here.

It may well be that the annual letters honed my skepticism of anything the government says. This skepticism characterizes the group of people who have been called, mistakenly to my mind, "the new historians." It would be more precise to call them "the first historians." Because during Israel's early years there was no historiography; there was mythology, there was ideology. There was a lot of indoctrination. When, at the beginning of the 1980s, the first historians were allowed to examine newly declassified documents, they found themselves time and again clutching their heads in amazement. *That's* not what we were taught in school, they said over and over. Then they prepared themselves for their critics: Why are you shattering our myths? Who gave you the right? Some people need myths—that's legitimate. But some say myths should not be examined because it's unpatriotic to do so. That's how it is with patriots—they always know who's a patriot and who isn't. I think part of Yehoshua's rage at those Rehavia teenagers was that they weren't patriotic enough for him.

When his fury subsided for a moment, I dared to ask what was wrong with talking about Volkswagens. I remember he told me I was abnormal. Maybe he was right, but some years later he would write:

When peace comes and the normative framework of the State of Israel wins the final recognition of the community of nations, and especially of the people of the region in which we live, we will know that normality is not pejorative. On the contrary, a new era of many possibilities will open in which the Jewish people can shape its own fate, create its own full culture, and participate in the shaping of mankind as a member with equal rights in the community of nations.

Normality will be revealed as the best way of being one and different, unique and special (like every other nation) without always fearing the loss of identity.

This, indeed, is the essence of the Zionist dream—a normal existence for the Jewish people, living in an independent country in which a majority of the citizens are Jews.

Most of Israel's citizens are Jews, yet nearly all of them have trouble agreeing on the fundamental norms of their society. In fact, they don't even agree on who is a Jew. This argument is not new—its roots run deep. In the deliberately ungrammatical words of the late Jerusalem philosopher Shmuel Hugo Bergmann, the argument is one between "two Jewish nation." Bergmann explained: "Judaism has always had two dueling factions. One is separatist. It hates the non-Jew. It fosters an Amalek complex"—the Amalekites attacked the Israelites from the rear during their desert sojourn, so God ordered their obliteration. "At every opportunity," Bergmann continues, this faction "stresses: 'Remember what he did to thee.' Then there is another Judaism, one that I would perhaps characterize with the verse 'Thou shalt love thy neighbor as thyself.' The prayer of that Judaism allows us to forget Amalek; it is a Judaism of love and forgiveness."

The Zionist movement never represented all the Jewish people. Israeli Zionism had a different set of interests than the Zionism represented by Theodor Herzl, the movement's Austro-Hungarian founder. The Zionist dream has always produced turbulent ideological, political, and moral disagreement. Among other contradictions, the reestablishment of the Jewish nation in its land was not only an act of transcendent historical justice; it also prompted war, displacement, grief, and misery.

This double-edged reality has generated millions of words in books, articles, and speeches, fueling a debate that has been going on in the State of Israel since the day it was founded. The debate burned even fiercer in 1998, as the country's fiftieth Independence Day approached. It's doubtful whether the argument fought at that moment produced a single new idea, but a new term, *post-Zionism*, made a frequent appearance. Mostly, the phrase is a slur—right-wingers use it to prove they are better patriots than the people on the left. As an insult, *post-Zionism* is thrown around to denounce everything from a willingness to compromise in the Israeli-Arab conflict to the challenges historians have posed to Zionism's historical myths.

But the term *post-Zionism* is also used as an evaluation of Zionism itself: it means that Zionism has done its job, with notable success, and that Israel must now move on to the next stage. Some see this as a goal and others see it as a threat. There is no easy agreement on who is a "post-Zionist" because there's no easy agreement on who is a Zionist. "It's probably even harder to define who is a Zionist than it is to define who is a Jew," Shmuel Ettinger, a historian, once said. This difficulty weighs down the discussion. The boundaries are blurred: Jew, Hebrew, Zionist, Israeli.

The debate goes on against the background of the dramatic changes Israel has undergone since the founding of the state. As Israelis have come to feel more secure, and as they have created a particularly Israeli way of life, Israel has become more "American" and more receptive to its Jewish traditions. These changes seemed to lead the country into a new situation, often referred to as a "post-Zionist" stage of development. At the beginning of 2000, this evolvement was given clear expression by the two men in the country who held the most political power: Chief Justice Aharon Barak, who, through the legal system, was working for a more American Israel, and Rabbi Ovadia Yosef, who, through his proxies in the Knesset, was working for a more Jewish Israel. Later that year, the "post-Zionist stage of development" found further expression in Israel's willingness to make substantial concessions to the Palestinians and share control over Jerusalem. But the outbreak of violence following the failure of negotiations halted the post-Zionist momentum.

Former prime minister Benjamin Netanyahu has observed that under the influence of Palestinian terror, Israel has moved from post-Zionism to post-post-Zionism, meaning a retreat to the past. Regrettably, he may be right. But Netanyahu's wit might merely reflect that the country once again is grappling with the ideology bequeathed by Theodor Herzl. This essay charts the many shifts and transformations of that ideology. It's a fascinating story.

Facing
Herzl's Statue

"All That Stuff Was Zionism"

On a hill above the Tel Aviv–Haifa highway at the Herzliya junction, there is a statue of Theodor Herzl, the town's name-sake. Resembling a silhouette, it is the Herzliya municipal-ity's contribution to raising Zionist consciousness. Uri Lifschitz, the sculptor, turned out a pretty ludicrous Herzl: the image is as flat as a wood shaving; Herzl is dressed in a black frock coat and looms above a water tower. To keep him from tipping over, he's secured in place with steel wire.

A few years after it was erected, the sculpture was repaired, and for the duration of the renovation a sign hung from the water tower, emblazoned with the contractor's name: Mohammed Mahamid, an Israeli-Arab. When the repairs were complete, the original legend reappeared under the sculpture: "Herzliya, a dream of a city," referring to the most famous statement attributed to Herzl, the prophet of Jewish statehood: "If you will it, it is no dream."

The history of Zionism proves that statement. In one hundred years of activity the Zionist movement led a part of the Jewish people to partial independence in a part of the Land of Israel, and for all the downside, it's a success story.

A yearning for the Land of Israel has attended the Jews always. It's a central subject in their writings from the Bible onward and a component of Jewish identity. In every country and at every time Jews have believed in the Exodus from Egypt to the land of Israel and the giving of the Torah. They knew of the kingdom of Israel, the Babylonian exile, and the oath of those exiles: "If I forget thee, O Jerusalem, may my right hand forget her cunning." Year after year they vowed, "Next year in Jerusalem." Most Jews didn't actually try to return to the Land of Israel; it was a religious object of desire, often an abstract spiritual concept, not a geographical destination they would actually consider moving to.

The first Zionist colonies were established in Palestine at the end of the nineteenth century, but only a handful of Jews settled in them. The Zionist enterprise received a big push forward when the movement succeeded in obtaining the support of the British Empire. Britain gained Palestine during World War I and ruled it for thirty years. Israel's collective memory tends to emphasize the struggle against the British regime. Among other things, the British are remembered for the restrictions they placed on Jewish immigration and land purchases. They are accused of support for the Arabs and animosity toward the Jews. Jewish terrorist actions against the British are depicted as a war of liberation.

A larger view gives a different picture. The British opened Palestine to mass Jewish immigration, and the Jewish population increased more than tenfold. The Zionist movement was allowed to purchase land, engage in agriculture, and establish hundreds of new settlements, including several cities—Herzliya was one of them. Palestine's Jews established elected political institutions, an army, and an economic infrastructure, including industrial plants and banks. The Zionist movement was allowed to establish an independent school system. These schools, and a large number of other public institutions, promoted Hebrew culture and a local national identity. All these helped the Jews defeat the Arabs and establish the State of Israel.

Israel is one of the great accomplishments of the twentieth century, despite its imperfections. During its early years, to live in Israel was to live in a state of gnawing anxiety. There was a pervasive feeling that everything was transitory and who knew whether two years from now there would even be a country. That's the explanation for the odd custom that Israeli passengers on El Al flights adopted: when an airplane landed in Tel Aviv, they would all break out in applause. The working assumption was that the plane would crash. Landing safely was cause for celebration.

The difficulties were in fact enormous. Israel overcame most of them. Very few people still applaud El Al pilots when the plane lands. There are third- and fourth-generation Israelis; they speak Hebrew with their parents, go to the same schools their parents went to, serve in the same army units, have the same experiences. They have a common way of life, a common sense of humor, common expectations. Today's Israeli children have something their parents and parents' parents often didn't have: living and proximate grandparents. That this ostensibly simple fact has become banal is the country's greatest achievement.

Israel defends its citizens. From time to time there are terrorist attacks, but generally the state provides its inhabitants with personal security. The Web sites of the UN, the World Bank, the International Monetary Fund, the World Health Organization, and UNESCO show that most Israelis are far better off than most of the people in the world. The data tables generally include about 150 countries; they compare measures such as GNPs, infant mortality rates, life expectancies, and literacy. Israel is in the top twenty on all such indexes. The standard and quality of life granted its citizens places it alongside several European countries. Most Israelis are better off each year, and this trend is continuing despite the widening gap between rich and poor. Most Israelis can thus assume that their children will have better lives than they have had, just as their own lives have been better than those of their parents.

Theodor Herzl's statue at the entrance to the city that bears his name looks out over an array of tall glass-and-steel office buildings. They are breathtakingly ostentatious, exuding success and luxury. Most of their tenants are giant high-tech companies, both Israeli and international, all in the spirit of the prophet: he dreamed of a flourishing urban culture. Herzliya has fancy stores and exclusive restaurants of the kind that Herzl himself craved. The stores have names like Tophouse, Columbus, and Beverly Hills, and there's a McDonald's as well. It's all in the spirit of the American century that Herzl heralded, including the Mizra Delicatessen, which sells pork-based cold cuts produced by a northern kibbutz. Its spacious salesroom is a kind of Shrine of Bacon offering imported tidbits from all over the world. Huge crowds of Israelis shop there; on Saturdays every parking place in the vicinity is taken. Herzl would have been thrilled. Actually, if Herzl lived in Israel today, he too might be attacked as a post-Zionist. In many ways, in fact, Herzl was the first post-Zionist.

Herzl believed that the Jews needed their own country because most of them could not live in their countries of residence as equal citizens. He saw persecution of and discrimination against the Jews as an immutable fact. So long as Jews lived in the Diaspora, they would be the victims of anti-Semitism. That is the Jewish problem. Herzl described two possible solutions: assimilation or emigration to another country where the Jews could establish a state of their own. Herzl did not believe in assimilation. So he called for a Jewish state.

Herzl recognized that the Land of Israel was the ancient and inalienable historical homeland of the Jews, but he seems to have stressed its merits largely as a way of marketing his

Zionist idea and capturing the hearts of the Jewish public. For his part, he didn't think the State of Israel necessarily had to be established in the Land of Israel. As far as he was concerned, Argentina was a definite possibility; he lauded it as one of the world's richest countries, with a huge territory, a sparse population, and a temperate climate. Late in his life, Herzl's diplomatic activity led the British Empire to offer the Jewish people national autonomy in East Africa—the territory under offer was mistakenly identified as Uganda. Herzl favored accepting the offer, at least as a temporary arrangement.

The first Arab protests against Zionism's aspirations were voiced while Herzl was still alive. Given his worldview, he might well have taken the view that the Land of Israel was not worth the price of war—Argentina might have been much simpler. He was also aware of the opposition the Zionist idea aroused in the Christian world and agreed that Jerusalem should not be included in the territory of the Jewish state. Herzl did not even place much value on the Hebrew language. "Who among us knows Hebrew well enough to use the language to ask for a train ticket?" he wrote. He supposed that the Jews in Israel would all speak their native languages. Switzerland was his example. He imagined his Jewish state as a nation of Jewish immigrants: "In the Land of Israel, too, we will remain what we are now, just as we will never cease to love, with regret and longing, the countries of our birth from which we were expelled," he wrote. That's exactly what happened, to the disgruntlement of some of the founding fathers of Israeli Zionism.

Menachem Begin wrote that the Jewish state was established thanks to Herzl's book *The Jewish State*, but this fundamental text of the Zionist movement articulates a Zionism that many Israelis have not adopted. One the whole, the founding fathers who settled in Palestine cultivated a local breed of Zionism that was very different from Herzl's. The most important difference between this homegrown ideology and Herzl's is that at a certain point the Zionists in Palestine ceased to view the establishment of the state as a means for solving the world Jewish problem and began to see it as an independent, and local, goal.

In comparison with Israeli Zionism, then, Herzl's Zionism comes out looking somewhat dim, pale, moderate, and compromising, really not at all patriotic—exactly what the Israeli political right now identifies as post-Zionist. Herzl would probably not have been surprised by this. From the start, most of the people who attacked his Zionist creed were Jews: religious Jews, liberals, and Marxists. Jewish opposition to Zionism is hardly a new Israeli invention; it has dogged the Zionist movement from its very beginnings. Until Israel was established, in fact, most Jews were not Zionists. And after its establishment, Israelis agreed to compromise on a fairly fuzzy, almost post-Zionist definition of their identity.

Zionism's first enemies were ultra-Orthodox Jews. Their rabbis viewed Zionism as heresy, feared that it endangered the Jews, and estimated that it was liable to challenge their position as the primary communal leaders. On the eve of the first Zionist Congress in 1897, the national organization of German rabbis condemned Zionism and stated that it ran counter to the messianic destiny of Judaism as expressed in the Holy Scriptures and other religious texts. The principal theological argument against Zionism was that the political effort to lead the Jews out of their Exile was "forcing the end." In other words, it created an artificial replacement for God and the true redemption. In doing so, they said, it violated the Jewish people's vow to wait patiently for the complete redemption that would come in the days of the Messiah, which depended entirely on the will of God. The Exile had acquired a halo of sanctity. Making frequent references to false messiahs of the past, the rabbis described Zionism as "the war of the evil urge," nothing but deception. "God forbid we should follow those sinners," they warned with a vehemence that had until then been reserved solely for Jews who had converted to Christianity.

Alongside the Talmudic injunction not to "mount the wall"—which was taken to mean a prohibition against organizing mass immigration to the Holy Land—ultra-Orthodox leaders also cited the injunction against violating any law of the lands of the Jewish Diaspora. The demand that Jews wait passively, while maintaining a low public profile, was founded not only in the rabbis' religious views but also in their responsibility for the safety of a small, weak religious minority that was always and everywhere confronted with discrimination, deportation, and violence. In the rabbis' opinion, Zionism was liable to be viewed as rebellion and nationalist agitation against the supreme authority of the countries in which the Jews resided. Such a perception, they feared, would endanger the entire Jewish community, both Zionism's supporters and its opponents.

But Zionism was also perceived as a competitor to religion, as subversion against rabbinical authority, because it promoted a new, secular Jewish identity. Zionism did not invent national Jewish secularism; that had emerged under the influence of changes in the societies in which the Jews of Europe lived. Nor did the Jewish identity fostered by the Zionist movement necessarily require a rejection of religious principles. But the political organizational activity of the Zionist movement threatened the religious establishment's monopoly. A number of rabbis overcame this ostensible contradiction between Judaism and Zionism, founding the religious Zionist movement.

The Zionism that Herzl represented was anchored in the liberal nationalism then blossoming in Europe, which quite naturally attracted many Jews. But this same perspective led many Jews to the conclusion that the only way for them to be recognized as citizens with equal rights was to integrate into the liberal national society taking shape around them. Jewish liberalism thus offered its own solution to the Jewish problem, one opposed to the Zionist solution. The desire to become integrated as equals into the countries of the Diaspora, yet still to preserve religious identity, encouraged a "reform" of Judaism that was expressed principally in forms of worship. Many

Reform Jews also saw Zionism as a threat to their status in the countries in which they lived.

At the dedication of a Reform synagogue in Charleston, South Carolina in 1841 one of the speakers declared, "The United States is our Land of Israel, this city is our Jerusalem, and this house of God is our Temple." There were those who gave up religion entirely or even accepted Christianity. Their goal was to eliminate the difference between them and their neighbors. Zionist ideology imposed otherness on them, labeling them as Jewish nationals. One of the high points of this dispute was the confrontation between two ministers in the British government, both of them Jewish: Herbert Samuel, a Zionist, and Edwin Montagu, his cousin.

Samuel served as postmaster general and later home secretary and was the first British high commissioner in Palestine. In 1917 he was among the driving forces behind the British declaration of support for the Zionist movement, known as the Balfour Declaration. Montagu, minister of munitions and then secretary of state for India, did his best to prevent the declaration from being issued. He rejected the claim that the Jews are a nation. The demand that they be recognized as having a distinct national identity threatened to hinder their struggle to become equal citizens of the countries in which they resided. In an emotional and touching letter Montagu sent to his prime minister, David Lloyd-George, he wrote that if the Land of Israel were declared the national home of the Jewish people, every antisemitic organization and newspaper would ask by what right a Jew served as a minister in the British government.

"The country for which I have worked ever since I left the University—England—the country for which my family have fought," Montagu wrote, "tells me that my national home, if I desire to go there, therefore my natural home, is Palestine." He presumed that the non-Jewish world would support Zionism in the hope of getting rid of all its Jews. Theodor Herzl also thought of this possibility but, unlike Montagu, welcomed it: "The anti-Semites will be our most loyal friends; the anti-Semitic countries will be our allies," he wrote in his diary. There were those who denied that the Jews were a nation, and there were those who assigned the Jews a historic mission as exiles and saw their dispersal among the peoples of the world as a cultural and ethical ideal.

Many Jews believed that the Jewish problem would be solved in the framework of a new order, in the spirit of Marxist ideology. The Zionist movement did not reject socialist principles; indeed, the Zionist labor movement led the Jewish community in Palestine to its victory. But many believed that to be truly class-conscious, one had to sacrifice one's national identity. The Marxist movement in Europe allowed Jews to be active in its ranks and even to reach prominent leadership positions. Jews stood out among the leaders of the Bolshevik Revolution in Russia and in a number of social-democratic parties. There was also a Jewish Marxist movement, the Bund, an influential competitor to the Zionist movement.

Alongside criticism from without, the Zionist movement also had to deal with differences of opinion among its members. Rival parties were formed that represented not only competing interests and sides in power struggles, but also worldviews that ranged from the far right to the far left. From the very first, opinions differed not just on tactics but also on fundamental questions, including the movement's goals and its way of achieving them. Early on, debates raged over the question of who was a Jew and who was a Zionist. Ahad Ha'am, the writer and thinker and Herzl's in-house rival, believed that it was enough to establish a "spiritual center" in Palestine. He opposed the creation of a politically sovereign state. There were those who reasoned that Zionism ought to fight for the rights of Jews in their countries of residence, whereas others believed that it should not. They argued over whether people could be Zionists without leaving their country of origin, or whether only a person who settled in the Land of Israel was a true Zionist.

Contrary to the prevailing wisdom in Israel today, the Zionist movement's principal opponents were thus Jews. The movement did not succeed in convincing most of the Jewish people that it was viable, and that was its great failure. By the time most Jews in the world had identified with Zionism's objectives, the movement had suffered a series of heavy blows.

Most Jews who settled in Israel did not do so because they were Zionists. They came as refugees, despite the fact that they were not Zionists. The same was also true, to a certain extent, of those who came in the earliest waves of immigration. The Zionist movement could tell itself that it had been proven right—Israel had become the place of refuge for persecuted Jews. True, but that could not change the fact that most of those who settled in the country came reluctantly. Most of them had trouble cutting themselves off from their past lives in the Exile. Nine out of every ten pioneers who came in the Second Aliya, the wave of immigration in the decade following 1905, ended up leaving the country.

For about ten years after settling in Palestine, writer Mordechai Ben-Hillel Hacohen, a delegate to the first Zionist Congress and whose daughter was married to Ahad Ha'am's son, continued to read *Die Jüdische Rundschau*, the German-Jewish newspaper. He was ecstatic when he had a chance to pore through Russian newspapers reporting the events of the Communist revolution. "What wonders are being done there in that country, in our near-far homeland!" he wrote in his diary. He feared that once granted equality, the Jews of Russia would not come to settle Palestine; they would no longer have any reason to leave. But when he read that the Russian czar had abdicated his crown and that a provisional government had been established, he wrote in his diary, "Our redemption is near, our complete redemption!" It was as if he were living on the Dnieper rather than near the Yarkon River in Tel Aviv.

In the 1920s refugees from the economic crisis in Poland arrived, in what was called the Fourth Aliya. Many, perhaps most, settled in Palestine because the United States was closed to them. In the 1930s it was the turn of refugees from Nazi Germany to arrive. The majority of participants in this Fifth Aliya would have preferred to remain in their own country or to emigrate elsewhere; they remained a generation of immigrants. Many of them had trouble breaking free from their sense of loss. Playwright Ya'akov Shabtai in his wistful comedy *Striped Tiger* wrote the following words for Shoshana, the owner of a small restaurant on the Tel Aviv beach in the 1930s: "If I had stayed there I could have gone to the Academy and I'd have long since been in the opera." The author's stage directions specify that the frustrated diva should be wearing a foxskin stole. The Tel Aviv heat was not hers.

The longing for the "old country" grew stronger whenever life in Israel became harsher and more demanding and the disparity between reality and expectations greater. Many passed this feeling on to their children. The latter internalized it without always being aware of its origin. This is the source of the heavy baggage carried by the phrase *hutz la'aretz*, "overseas." Most of the world's inhabitants live in poverty under authoritarian regimes, but when Israelis say "overseas" they mean a standard of living and culture that is higher than at home. Long before anyone spoke of post-Zionism, in the 1920s, 1930s, 1950s, and 1960s, many Israelis left their country. Few did so because they'd read a post-Zionist book published by some professor. They left because it was hard to live in Israel. Often those who emigrated continued, in their new homes, to consider themselves Israeli and Zionist.

Some of the Zionist movement's ideologues, especially

those from the labor movement, attributed a moral purpose to Zionism. Inspired by other Jewish writers who were not necessarily Zionists, these ideologues described life in the Diaspora as degenerate and parasitic. It was, they wrote, a life based on trading, brokering, and moneylending. They believed that the consummation of Zionist ideology would lead to a revolution in values. Unlike Herzl's brand, Zionism in Palestine cultivated profound scorn, even rancor, toward Jewish life in the Exile and Jewish culture. Then after the slaughter of the Jews during World War II became known one Zionist newspaper in Palestine wrote: "Had the [Nazi] enemy succeeded in striking at us in *this* place, it would have been a blow that extinguished the soul. The destruction would certainly have been much smaller in quantity than the destruction of Jewish Europe, but in quality and historical significance it would have been much greater." In a meeting between Prime Minister David Ben-Gurion and a group of writers not long after the state was established, the poet Leah Goldberg said of the Jews, "This people is ugly, mediocre, morally deranged, and difficult to love."

The "rejection of the Exile" led the Zionist labor movements ideologues to devise an ideal "new Jew," or "new man" they sought to create in the Land of Israel, at times through coercion. Aharon Appelfeld, a novelist, has written about a boy, an immigrant from Poland, whose classmates bullied and beat him up because he could not suntan as they did. The boy assured them that he was trying as hard as he could to make his skin darker, but they believed that had he really wanted to change, he would have done so. His pale skin seemed to bring the Exile and the Holocaust to them, so they beat him up. The people who ran the immigrant camps of the 1950s similarly tried to impose a secular Israeli identity on Yemenite children, forcing them to cut off their sidelocks.

The dream of a "new man" was borrowed from ideas that were then in vogue in the Soviet Union, Weimar Germany, and Fascist Italy. There were those who spoke of a "new Jewish race." Ze'ev Jabotinsky, leader of right-wing Revisionist Zionism, spoke of "a new psychological race of Jew." In this context, the term *Jew* was often eschewed in favor of *Hebrew*. The new Hebrew, the opposite of the Diaspora Jew, was supposed to skip over two-thousand years of exile and connect directly with the heroes of the Bible. In posters and in photographs he was depicted as a muscular, light-haired, happy youth. The young Israeli man is superior in every respect to the young Jewish man of the Diaspora, claimed one of the leaders of the local educational system: "He is erect, brave, handsome, well-developed in his body, loves work, sport, and games; he is free in his movements, devoted to his people and its patrimony." He was frequently depicted as a farmer; being close to the land was considered truly Zionist. City life and, often, theoretical studies, including university, were not.

Working the land was meant to fortify the Yishuv, the Jewish community in Palestine. It was also considered a moral obligation, a "religion of labor," as it was sometimes called. An article in the newspaper *Ha'aretz* stated of the graduates of the Ben-Shemen Agricultural School, "They will bring pure and clean blood to our national labor, the labor of the land." The children of Palestine's farming settlements were living, in the view of Zionist leader Chaim Weizmann, "the original Hebrew life." At times working the land was described in almost erotic terms by, among others, poet Chaim Nachman Bialik. Agricultural workers, he wrote, "empty the strength of their youth into the bowels of this blasted ground in order to bring it to life." Moshe Smilansky, a farmer and writer, said that living in Tel Aviv was like living in a huge hotel and warned that "the shopkeeping mentality" would lead the city's residents to "hucksterism, assimilation, and apostasy," not national revival. "Store after store," carped another commentator, hotel after hotel, pensions, hairdressers, soft drink stands, kiosks. Soft drink vendors were a popular and disparaging symbol for immigrants who preferred the convenience of city life to farming. One writer in *Ha'aretz* referred to the "horrible scourge" of interest-charging moneylenders and "all sorts of other blood-sucking leeches." When people wanted to prophesy the most dire, horrible future imaginable, they predicted that someday Tel Aviv would have a stock exchange. The goal was to "obliterate the memory of the city."

Nevertheless, the society that arose in Israel was manifestly urban, similar to that characteristic of Jewish life in the Diaspora. As in the Diaspora, most Jews in Israel did not engage in production. They were traders, middlemen, and members of the other professions typical of Jews elsewhere. The phenomenon only became more pronounced. In the mid-1950s, 16 percent of Israelis worked in agriculture. By the mid-1990s that figure had dropped to 3 percent. Kibbutz members claimed to be the Zionist elite and, until the Six Day War, acted as the movement's caretakers. They played a large role in marking out the country's borders, but the focus of Zionist activity was in Tel Aviv, not in the kibbutzim.

The Zionist enterprise in the Land of Israel required the establishment of a Jewish majority, and that meant increasing the Jewish population. At the beginning of 1921, after the first serious clashes between Jews and Arabs in Palestine, *Ha'aretz* made an emotional plea to the world's Jews: "Do not leave us alone at the front. Do not slight the blood of the pioneers you sent before the nation! Come to us in your masses, come to us in your multitudes to strengthen the Hebrew position, to bring us more working hands, hands for defense!"

In the wake of one of the first attacks on Palestine's Jews, Joseph Klausner, a historian, wrote: "If the Arabs imagine that they can provoke us to war and that because we are few they will easily win, they are making a huge error. Our campaign will include all 13 million Jews in all the countries of the world. And everyone knows how many statesmen, how many opinion makers, how many people of great wisdom and great wealth and great influence we have in Europe and America." This statement was one of the first indications of the about-face that would take place among Palestine's Zionists. Instead of seeing the state as a means of saving the world's Jews, they demanded that the world's Jews defend the community in Palestine.

The theoretical obligation to world Jewry ostensibly remained unchanged. When the Zionists demanded that world Jewry reinforce the community in Palestine and finance the Zionist project, the movement's leaders acted on the assumption that the settlers were functioning as a vanguard and were building the state that would in time take in the entire people. In June 1938, Ben-Gurion wrote, "The purpose for which the Jewish state will be established is to absorb a maximum number of immigrants and in doing so to aid in solving the question of the Jewish people in the world." The state was meant to "redeem" the world's Jews and to realize their right to return to their homeland. At the same time, Ben-Gurion also said that he did not oppose saving Jews in other countries "despite our Zionist ideology." But in fact he tended to see attempts to aid Jews elsewhere as harmful competition. He attacked, for instance, the Joint Distribution Committee, a welfare organization that worked worldwide and was not subordinate to the Zionist movement. This is the background to Ben-Gurion's view of the international conference that convened in Évian, France, to discuss the Jewish refugee problem. He warned that opening other countries to Jewish immigration was liable to thwart the Zionist demand that they be sent to Palestine.

The British authorities gave the Zionist movement a virtually free hand in choosing which Jews would be allowed to settle in Palestine. The movement's representatives chose its candidates carefully. The first preference was for young men. Even during European Jewry's worst travails, the leadership of the Jewish Agency—the Jewish independent administration in Palestine—preferred to prevent the arrival of the elderly and ill. In a few cases it even sent people back to Nazi Germany because they had become a burden on the community in Palestine.

The Zionist enterprise also depended to a large extent on Jews being willing to fund it. Ben-Gurion was concerned that the persecution in Europe would affect the movement's ability to raise money for development in Palestine. "While myriads of Jewish refugees are languishing and suffering in concentration camps, even the Zionists among them will not respond to the needs of Palestine," he wrote. Less than two weeks after the beginning of World War II, he declared that "the fate of the Land of Israel hangs in the balance." The distance between the perceptions of the community in Palestine and those of the rest of the Jewish world, and between the ideas of Herzlian Zionism and those of the Yishuv were by this time profound.

The persecution of the Jews leading to World War II had forced the Zionist movement to face a truth it had tried to repress. Palestine could not solve the Jewish problem in Europe, a fact that became ever more clear as Arab opposition to the Zionist project increased. At least two Zionist leaders, Max Nordau and Ze'ev Jabotinsky, proposed transporting Jews to Palestine in large rescue operations. There was no practical possibility of doing this, not only because the British prohibited mass immigration, but also because the country could not absorb refugees at such a pace. In 1934 Ben-Gurion said that Palestine had room for 4 million Jews. Two years later he spoke of "at least" 8 million. Some spoke of bringing 50,000 Jews a year; others spoke of 100,000 Jews a year. At that rate the process would have taken between fifty and one hundred years, and even then just half the world's Jews, at most, would be living in Palestine. In 1937 Ben-Gurion talked about bringing 1.5 million Jews, explaining that this was vital in order to create a Jewish majority. That would have taken fifteen years. Toward the end of the war, Ben-Gurion spoke of the need to bring over 1 million Jews "immediately."

None of these figures would have saved most of the Jews who were persecuted in Europe. The tragedy of Zionism in a nutshell is that while it may have foreseen the catastrophe, the solution it offered was irrelevant. Furthermore, prior to the establishment of the state the Zionist movement did not have the functional ability to organize mass rescue operations. The first rescue it mounted after the Nazis came to power was through an agreement made with the Third Reich allowing German Jews to take a large part of their property with them to Palestine.

At a later date it became common wisdom that had the State of Israel been established in 1937, in accordance with the British partition plan, it would have prevented the Holocaust. There is no reason to think so. In half a century of independence Israel has not yet absorbed 6 million Jewish immigrants. The movement did manage to get several thousand out of occupied Europe; perhaps it could have rescued more. The Zionists certainly could not have rescued millions, and in fact only a relatively small portion of the Holocaust's survivors owed their lives to the movement's rescue efforts. The story of the Zionist movement during the Holocaust is one of helplessness.

The archives preserve the words of one Jewish Agency rescue worker in Istanbul. Only a small number of people relative to the magnitude of the catastrophe had been saved, he estimated, but those who escaped came out as Zionists, with their eyes set on Palestine. "We have saved their souls," another rescue worker comforted himself. In this spirit the Zionist movement argued that a large majority of the Holocaust survivors in displaced persons camps after the war wanted to settle in Palestine. There is good reason to doubt that. The choice facing the refugees was Palestine or a return to their countries of origin in Eastern and Central Europe, to devastated, starving cities and to communism and anti-Semitism. But for a handful of exceptions, the survivors were not given a choice between Palestine and the United States. Quite naturally, they chose Palestine. Most of the refugees, physically and mentally ravaged, were nothing like the Yishuv leaders' hopes. "At first I thought they were animals," wrote one of the first emissaries to reach the camps. But the main question on Ben-Gurion's mind was "Where will we get people for Israel?"

Ideological bewilderment and shame at the failure of its rescue efforts were only the lighter part of the blow the Holocaust dealt to the Zionist movement. The real catastrophe was the loss of the population that had been designated for a Jewish majority in Palestine—the population of Europe.

• • •

The Zionist movement was born in Europe, drew its inspiration from Europe and was part of its history. Zionism's romantic nationalism, liberalism, and socialism all came from Europe. The movement's founding figures had assigned it a cultural mission. The Jewish state in the Land of Israel, Theodor Herzl wrote, would serve Europe as a defensive wall against Asia: "We can be the vanguard of culture against barbarism." Max Nordau asserted that the Jews would not lose their European culture in Palestine, nor would they adopt the inferior culture of Asia, just as the British had not turned into Indians in America or Papuans in Australia. "We will endeavor to do in the Near East what the English did in India. . . . It is our intention to come to Palestine as the representatives of culture and to take the moral boundaries of Europe to the Euphrates River," Nordau said at one of the Zionist Congresses. In their contacts with the British government, Zionist leaders continually emphasized that the Jewish state would be a cultural outpost for Europe. Thus European culture was meant to constitute part of the essence of the New Hebrew.

Practically, the Zionist movement could not lay the foundations for a state on its own. It had to hitch its fate to one of the empires, and the British Empire's sponsorship created the impression that the Zionists were settling in Palestine as agents of colonialism. Ironically, Zionist leaders in Palestine were furious at British administrators, who classified them as *natives,* an insulting colonialist term. The Zionists maintained that the natives were the Arabs; they, the Zionists, represented European culture.

They defined their European self-image not only in opposition to their view of the Arabs but also in contrast to their view of the Jews of the Arab countries. In the early periods these were largely from Yemen. Before the news of the slaughter of Europe's Jews reached the Zionist movement, it took little interest in the Jews of the Arab world. "We have been accustomed to see the Jews of the East largely as a subject for historical and anthropological study," a Zionist leader said. According to Ben-Gurion, they had not "noticed" the Jews of the Orient. "We came here as Europeans," Ben-Gurion said. "Our roots are in the East and we are returning to the East, but we bear with us the culture of Europe."

The Holocaust forced Zionism to bring Jews from the Arab world to the new country. Taking them in was a blow to its self-image and to its cultural aspirations, so the Zionist leadership did not bring oriental Jews to Israel eagerly, but because there was no other choice. "Israel needs working and fighting hands," said one of the first government ministers. As a result, even at the beginning of the 1950s, the Israeli government conducted a policy of selecting immigrants useful to the state, "good human material." It also regulated the rate of immigration in accordance with the country's needs, which did not necessarily match the needs of Jews in other countries.

There is no easy way to determine which of the oriental Jews came to Israel because they wanted to leave their countries of origin and which were forced to come by circumstances. Some were most likely inspired by one form or another of religious or political messianism, or a combination of the two.

Most likely, many joined other immigrants out of fear of being left behind. Very few had the opportunity to choose between immigration to Israel and to some other country. A large number left their homes because the Zionist struggle in Palestine did not allow them to remain; they had been identified, like it or not, as Zionists. At this point in its history, then, the Zionist movement did not serve as a solution to the Jewish problem. On the contrary, it led to the uprooting of entire Jewish communities.

Alongside the need to absorb the survivors of the Holocaust and the Jews of the Arab world, Israel was required to compromise with a new kind of Zionism that had its source largely in the United States. During Israel's early years, Ben-Gurion tried to maintain the position that a Jew who considered himself American, who did not feel that he lived in exile, was not a Zionist. Prime Minister Golda Meir asked, "Why aren't we allowed to say that the only Zionist is the one who packs up his belongings and moves to Israel?" She emphasized that "we cannot make peace with the thought" that "the Jewish Exile" would always exist. In the United States this exclusive approach was rejected.

Israel was forced to compromise with America's Jews because it needed their support. Ben-Gurion thus agreed that the decision to immigrate to Israel should be made freely by every individual. Israel and the Zionist movement invested effort and money in persuading Jews to immigrate, but after a long debate agreed to forgo the contention that the goal of Zionism was to gather in "all the exiles." Instead, its goal was "the ingathering of exiles." In time, it stopped referring to the *Exile* and began using a more neutral term, *Diaspora*. Zionist identity was thus reformulated in the United States, where Jews recognized the central position of the State of Israel and the duty to assist it, but without renouncing the need to care for Jews in other countries. Over the years, American Jewry has set aside larger and larger shares of the money it collects for Jewish projects in the United States, instead of sending the money to Israel.

Sometime after the Soviet Union severed diplomatic relations with Israel, the country put itself at the head of a worldwide struggle against the restrictions that the Soviet regime imposed on Jewish emigration. The fight was for the right of Soviet Jews to immigrate to Israel. But when Jews were allowed to leave, when the first cracks appeared in the Communist regime, it turned out that most of them by far preferred to settle in the United States—and that is what they did. These "dropouts," as they were called in Israel, were a most serious blow to Zionism's self-image and prestige. When it found itself almost without immigrants, Israel did what the Zionist movement had done after the Holocaust: it "discovered" Jews that until then had aroused at best folkloristic interest—the Jews of Ethiopia. Before the 1980s Israel had refused to take them in. But thereafter they were received with great enthusiasm, as if they were the saviors of the Zionist enterprise. Yet, within a very short time, the newcomers found themselves facing treatment that ranged from reserved to hostile. In the meantime, the Communist empire collapsed. Israel then demanded that the United States end the free immigration of Jews from the former Soviet Union because they were no longer political refugees. Since then, most Jews who have left the former Soviet Union have settled in Israel. But tens of thousands have chosen the only other country that gives preferential treatment to Jews: Germany.

These, then, are the struggles, the cracks, the compromises, and the long series of blows that the Zionist movement has had to endure over the years. Not one of them was the product of the rise of "post-Zionist" ideology. To this list may be added the conflict with the Arabs and a series of developments within Hebrew culture, some of which are manifestly anti-Zionist.

Arab resistance confronted the Zionist movement with a range of problems and ideas, both practical and political. The Zionists were never content with being strong; they insisted also on the justness of their cause. They did not want to conquer Palestine by force, but rather to receive it by right. In their efforts to be just and correct, in their own eyes and in the eyes of others, they frequently stressed that they were bringing good fortune and prosperity to all inhabitants of the land, both Jews and Arabs. In keeping with this notion of justice, the original idea was to try to purchase land, and indeed the Zionists legally bought part of Palestine's territory from its owners.

But war was inevitable. Israelis have looked back a thousand times in an effort to figure out where they erred and what should be done in order not to repeat the mistakes of the past.

No other subject has so preoccupied them. They made mistakes at certain junctures. Not every step they took was justified; not every position they adhered to was vital. But the only way to reach an agreement with the Arabs would have been to renounce the Zionist dream itself. Until Israel established itself as a military power whose survival was ensured, nothing could have brought the Arabs to allow the Zionist movement to create a Jewish majority even in a part of Palestine. The dispute was not territorial. It wasn't a debate over where the border would run, nor an argument over how governance should be structured and shared. It wasn't the Zionists' refusal to integrate into the culture of the East that prevented reaching an agreement, but rather the fundamental and absolute refusal of the Arabs to acquiesce in the Zionist enterprise itself. Resolution could be achieved only by force.

The Zionist movement at times depicted the Jews as a people without a land returning to a land without a people. Zionist historiography has cultivated the thesis that the settlers were shocked when they discovered that Palestine was inhabited by Arabs. The truth is that the movement's leaders knew very well there were Arabs in the country, and that they opposed the Zionists. From the beginning the Zionists knew their project would involve confrontation with the local population.

In fact, at the start of the twentieth century the Arabs were already saying nearly everything they would say in the hundred years that followed. One of the leaders of the Arab community in Jerusalem wrote to Theodor Herzl, "The world is big enough, there are other uninhabited lands in which millions of poor Jews could be settled. . . . in the name of God, leave Palestine alone!" That was in 1899. Two years later, Arab leaders signed a petition demanding the restriction of Jewish immigration to Palestine and a prohibition against their purchase of land, laying the foundations for the battle against Zionism. In 1905, Najib 'Azuri, one of the heralds of the Arab national movement, published a book in Paris. The awakening of the Arab people, 'Azuri wrote, was taking place simultaneously with the Jews' attempt to reestablish the ancient Israeli kingdom. The two movements were doomed to fight relentlessly until one defeated the other. The fate of the entire world depended on the outcome, he wrote.

Ahad Ha'am had already addressed the issue in his *Truth from Palestine,* published in 1891. Jewish settlers, he wrote, "treat the Arabs with hostility and cruelty, trespass unjustly, beat them shamelessly for no sufficient reason, and even take pride in doing so." He gave a psychological explanation for the phenomenon: "The Jews were slaves in the land of their Exile, and suddenly they found themselves with unlimited freedom, wild freedom that only exists in a land like Turkey." This sudden change had produced in their hearts an inclination toward repressive tyranny, as always happens "when a slave rules." Ahad Ha'am warned: "Outside Palestine, we are used to thinking of the Arabs as primitive men of the desert, as a donkey-like nation that neither sees nor understands what is going on around it . . . But should the time come when the life of our people in Palestine imposes to a smaller or greater extent on the natives, they will not easily step aside."

Others also wrote about the "Arab problem." It wasn't easy for the Zionists to explain to themselves and others that the conflict over the Land of Israel sometimes put the Jewish inhabitants of Palestine in danger, sometimes even in more danger than they would have faced in the Diaspora. Many Zionists also had difficulties resolving the contradiction between the movement's commitment to democratic values and the right of national self-determination on the one hand and their efforts, on the other hand, to impose a regime that was unwanted by a majority of the country's inhabitants. Most Zionists were not cynics; they believed in the justice of their cause and in European liberal values. For that reason they said that the Jews in Palestine spoke in the name of all the world's 17 million Jews, and that their status as a minority was but temporary, until the others arrived. The Land of Israel was the only country the Jews had, they said over and over again, while the Arabs had many lands. In keeping with this, the Zionist movement explored the possibility of funding the transfer of the Arab population, or at least a part of it, outside the borders of Palestine in the framework of "voluntary relocation," as they called it. Such a policy would create a Jewish majority and thus preserve Zionism's allegiance to democratic principles.

• • •

For a century, life in Palestine, then in Israel, swung between terrorism and war and war and terrorism. The confrontations during the British Mandate generated hatred, fear, and a view that the establishment of the Jewish state required removing the Arabs from the country. That happened in 1948: hundreds of thousands of Arabs left, fled, and were expelled from their homes to become destitute refugees. Most of them were not allowed to return. A large part of their lands and homes were confiscated. Those who remained became citizens of Israel and were permitted to vote for and be elected to the Knesset. In practice, they were not allowed to engage in free political activity. That was seen to by the military government imposed on them during the country's early years. The military regime was gradually withdrawn, but even after it was canceled a series of laws and arrangements remained in force that discriminated against Israel's Arabs.

The permanent state of war was the fuel that propelled Israel and the substance that held its people together in a single, mobilized, resilient society, tied by bonds of Zionist patriotism. To a large extent, it determined the structure of the economy and was the central element in Israeli self-consciousness and politics. Yet at the same time there were also voices raising questions about the basic goals of the Zionist movement. There was, of course, the ultra-Orthodox community, which never accepted Zionism and which was a not insignificant proportion of the public. During the Mandate period a number of important intellectuals, leaders in their fields—like Martin Buber—tried to promote various alternatives to the Zionist idea. These included Jewish integration into an Arab federation and the establishment of a joint Jewish-Arab state.

In such a binational state there would not be a Jewish majority, and in this it lay outside the fundamental principles of the Zionist platform. But the idea's supporters included the Hashomer Hatzair movement, one of the major forces on Israel's Zionist left. The idea of a binational state, and other ideas that departed from Zionist principles, were also current in Aliya Hadasha, a centrist party of mostly German immigrants that had the support of about 10 percent of the population.

One Saturday at the end of the 1920s, three young men sat on a bench on Allenby Street in Tel Aviv, chatting and smoking cigarettes. A religious Jew who passed by reproached them for smoking on the Sabbath. "But I'm not Jewish," one of the young men responded. His name was Uriel Halperin, who later became famous, under his pen name Yonatan Ratosh, as a poet and the prophet of the Canaanites. The epithet "Canaanites" was first applied to Ratosh and his Hebrew Youth movement by its opponents but was later adopted by the group itself. They considered themselves Hebrews, not Jews; they fought not only the Jewish religion but Zionism as well. They denied the existence of a Jewish people and believed that Muslims, Druze, and Christians could be members of the Hebrew nation. Their Hebrew chauvinism included patently fascist elements. But they found no political leader, never developed organizationally, and attracted only a handful of followers.

Yet the Canaanite worldview was more than an intellectual curiosity. It sustained a mood that was anchored in part in the new Hebrew consciousness that the Zionist movement itself had cultivated. It influenced an entire generation of young people who sought a Hebrew alternative to Zionism. It was the new Israeli identity of a number of writers and artists. One of their most visible representatives was a young German-born journalist named Uri Avneri.

Eight months after Israel declared its independence, Avneri published in *Ha'aretz* his "Confessions of a Young Hebrew," in which he invoked some of the innovative slang of the time, such as using the term "Zionism" to mean "vapid rhetoric;" the full phrase was "Zionism, in quotation marks." "The greatness [of the generation of 1948]," Avneri wrote, "has been its pragmatism. In the combat units, all the ideological slogans and phrases entirely disappeared. All that stuff was Zionism, stuff that had no content and was beside the point." Avneri tried to be the voice of a generation of fighters who had experienced the shock of returning from battle. In fact, he not only expressed an existing mood; to a large measure, he invented it, under the influence of a similar mood that was current among soldiers in Europe after World War I. A while later Avneri bought the weekly magazine *Haolam Hazeh* and became its editor.

Haolam Hazeh was more than a magazine. It united its readers into an elitist peer group and gave them an unmatchably flattering self-image. Avneri told them that the very fact that they read the magazine meant they were among the good and the righteous, the intelligent and the daring. He fortified their sense of being tomorrow's forces of light standing against yesterday's forces of darkness, the few versus the many. In doing so, Avneri created, over the years, an entire set of myths and images that existed only in the pages of his magazine, in a language and style that also existed only in the pages of his magazine. He constructed an imaginary world of heroes and villains, and his magazine was an object of adoration and disgust, of affection and anxiety.

Paradoxically, Avneri identified Zionism with the Diaspora mentality that native Israelis wanted no part of. Zionism was the opposite of the liberated, Hebrew identities of the Sabra generation, the cohort of young, native-born Israelis. More than anywhere else, this was expressed in *Haolam Hazeh*'s treatment of the Kastner affair at the beginning of the 1950s. Rudolf Kastner, a leader of the Budapest Jewish community and an activist in Mapai, the labor Zionist party led by Ben-Gurion, was the central witness in a libel trial growing out of accusations that he had collaborated with the Nazis. Avneri portrayed the affair as a battle between the old, cringing, submissive Diaspora Jewish mentality, represented by Kastner, and the young, upright, rebellious Hebrew—Mordechai the Jew of the Book of Esther versus Judah the Maccabee.

Along with his adoration of the Israel Defense Forces, the

Hebrew army, Avneri called for an alliance with the Arabs to be founded on the common "Semitic" identity of the Middle Eastern peoples. This, too, was a notable deviation from the prevailing Zionist identity. Avneri was among the first Israelis to call for the establishment of an Arab state in Palestine, alongside Israel.

Haolam Hazeh gave extensive coverage to and promoted a long succession of protest movements, among them Israel's Black Panthers, a group of young oriental Jews from disadvantaged neighborhoods, and Matzpen, a radical Trotskyite faction. Some of these movements engaged only in political and social protest, including criticism of Israel's military policy. Others, encouraged by Avneri, offered cultural alternatives, and some of them sought to challenge the Zionist idea itself. It was Avneri who later invented the term *post-Zionism.* As part of this philosophy, he frequently encouraged the publication of new historical revelations and challenged accepted historical truths.

Indeed, myths were being challenged long before the terms *new historians* and *post-Zionism* appeared. In the 1950s, the media were already publishing exposés about war crimes committed by Israeli soldiers during the War of Independence. There were also revelations about infighting between Zionist factions dating nearly to the dawn of the movement, on occasion leading to murder. The prevailing myth of the Yishuv's battle against the Nazi scourge was challenged in a book by Yoel Brand, a Zionist functionary who reported that the movement had conducted negotiations with Adolf Eichmann. Other writers chronicled Israel's discrimination against Jewish immigrants from the Arab world. Still others wrote less than complimentary biographies of mythic leaders or challenged the country's military policy. The publication of the diaries of former prime minister Moshe Sharett showed him to be a sharp critic of many of Ben-Gurion's policies, and Yitzhak Rabin's autobiography included a chapter—which was censored—on the expulsion of Arabs during the War of Independence.

Even ancient history was not spared. Reserve General Yehoshafat Harkabi wrote a book charging that Bar Kochba, the leader of the Jewish rebellion against Rome in 132–35, had been not a hero but a madman. He had, Harkabi claimed, led the Jewish people into a catastrophe comparable to the Holocaust.

Self-criticism and doubt, or what some call "a weakness of vision" up to and including defeatism and despair, have thus always been an inseparable part of Zionist history. Long before anyone invented post-Zionism, the movement was much weaker, and its influence much smaller, than many Israelis realize. It has always had to confront opinions that whittled away at both its ideology and its mythology.

FACING
ELVIS'S STATUE

"When They Start Shooting
I Start Missing New York"

At Neve Ilan, along the road to Jerusalem, there is a gas station. Next to the gas station is the Elvis Presley Diner. A few years ago the proprietors erected a glistening white, larger-than-life statue of the singer at the restaurant's entrance. The image bears a plaque noting the sculptor's name: Lance Hunter. This Elvis signals victory—the Bolshevism of the early Ben-Gurion years has been defeated. Israelis have chosen America.

The full story of the Americanization of Israel has yet to be told, even though it is central to the country's history. It can be summed up simply: ever-growing dependence on the United States in every area of life. Americanization has weakened social solidarity and, in contrast with original Israeli Zionism, has made the individual the centerpoint of life.

Once a year, on the eve of Independence Day, Israelis used

to go out to the streets to dance the hora to accordion music until dawn, re-creating the spontaneous joy of 1947 when the United Nations General Assembly voted to establish a Jewish state. Strangers would join hands in the circle dance that in Israeli poetry and literature symbolizes the unity of the collective.

As years have gone by, the custom has almost entirely vanished. Since the 1970s Israelis have preferred to celebrate at private parties or family picnics in parks or on the beach. Many of the holiday-makers buy little Israeli flags from boys who peddle them at road junctions, then they attach the flags to their car windows. In recent years one sees cars flying the American flag as well—also available at major intersections. "America," Zvi Sobel of the University of Haifa has written, "has become Israel's alter-ego, politically, economically, and culturally. America has become the teacher, the giant father figure hovering over us; in fact, it holds the keys to life in Israel, the keys of existence."

Some basic lines of the Israeli story are similar to those of America. In Israel, as in the United States, immigrants arrived in a country that was already partly inhabited. They pushed out and in many cases destroyed the local inhabitants. Both Israelis and Americans gained their independence fighting the British. In both places the revolution was supposed to express a commitment to universal values of freedom and justice, but in both places a long time passed before this ethical commitment became actual policy. Israeli democracy developed gradually; in its early years, Israel did not respect fundamental human rights and did not guarantee equal civil rights to all. During those same years the American democracy had not yet formally ended discrimination against blacks. In both places the flaws in democracy were papered over with self-righteous rhetoric.

Like the United States, Israel endeavored to be a social and moral melting pot, but in practice it established a new multicultural society. In time, assimilation even ceased to be a declared goal, and pluralism was praised. Sami Shalom Shitrit, a Moroccan-born teacher and poet, brought back the principle of multiculturalism from his studies in America. No more "absorption through modernization," which is what the founding fathers of Israeli sociology recommended to achieve a "blending of the exiles," but rather cultural separation. "Like the blacks in America, Sephardic Jews in Israel suffered discrimination at the hands of Western Ashkenazic Jews and must assert their own identities." He declared:

> In the United States, whose failures we faithfully imitate, but with a 20-year delay, blacks have begun to study history within their communities with a drastic change in approach. They teach history based on the reality of the street and the community, returning to African origins, via slave-hunting by whites, through the years of slave labor, the years of discrimination and racism, to today's continuation of the struggle.
>
> An American black child today learns American history from the point of view of the victim. He must undergo this

process in order to develop a full, unconflicted identity. I would adopt this approach without waiting 20 unnecessary years. . . .

Theodor Herzl wrote, "America will surely overtake Europe, just as a large estate swallows up a smaller one." He wrote this in response to Zionists who proclaimed that Jews who returned to their land should become farmers—an idea Herzl considered a peculiar error. The future after all belonged to industry, he believed, and he was right. The twentieth century, whose beginning coincided with the final years of Herzl's life, was the American century. All nations kept their eyes on the American experiment—not just the Zionists, and tried, to one degree or another, to emulate it.

Sometime after World War I broke out, Eliezer Ben-Yehuda left Palestine for a visit to the United States. Before leaving he deposited his manuscripts with the American consul in Jerusalem, Otis Glazebrook, to keep them safe. The work of this great Hebrew linguist laid the foundations for one of the Zionist movement's principal achievements: turning Hebrew into a spoken language. During the war the U.S. government sent assistance to the Jews of Palestine, almost certainly saving them from famine. Mordecai Ben-Hillel Hacohen recorded in his diary, "The entire national enterprise in Palestine has fallen on America's shoulders." The United States also assisted refugees from Palestine, and one of the Hebrew battalions that participated in the conquest of the Turks was mustered in America. Several of the Yishuv's public leaders who had been expelled by the Turks spent this period in the United States, among them Yitzhak Ben-Zvi, later Israel's second president, and David Ben-Gurion.

Michael Bar-On, who has written about the American sojourns of several Palestinian Jewish leaders, made note of the fact that they were involved principally in the life of the Jewish community. Yet Ben-Gurion, Ben-Zvi, and others were disappointed by the marginal interest American Jews took in them. Ben-Zvi complained that in America Zionism had become a leisure activity. He and his colleagues thought that the freedom offered by the United States negatively affected American Jews' willingness to enlist in the Zionist cause. "America will shorten our lives," Ben-Gurion wrote to a colleague. Their dependence on American Jewish aid made Yishuv figures feel even more hostile and scornful. The feelings were exacerbated by their principled commitment to socialism.

After the war there was a short-lived proposal that the United States, rather than Britain, receive the League of Nations Mandate for Palestine. The idea was soon filed away, but American involvement in the Middle East increased. Contrary to common wisdom, the United States and not Britain was the major power in the region. Ben-Gurion had been among the first to become cognizant of America's growing influence and of the need to focus the Zionist movement's major efforts on Washington and New York. The longer he pursued the American connection, the greater his standing grew, in comparison with Chaim Weizmann, who stuck to his conviction that the key to the future of Zionism lay in London. By the eve of Israeli independence Britain was a fairly marginal player—President Harry Truman was the pivotal man.

A few weeks after the declaration of independence, an American Jew named Fred Gronich appeared in Israel. Teddy Kollek, Israel's chargé d'affaires in Washington and an avid Americanophile, had referred him to Ben-Gurion. Gronich spent about a year and a half in Israel under an assumed name, Fred Harris. A short time after his arrival a rumor began spreading through the country: David Ben-Gurion had hired an American military adviser with the rank of colonel. *Kol Haam*, the Communist Party newspaper, accused the prime minister of treason.

Ben-Gurion frequently met with Gronich and from time to time invited him to meetings of the army's general staff. Gronich, he said, was superior to any other military expert he knew. Ben-Gurion frequently accepted his advice. It is doubtful whether anyone had a greater influence on the Israeli army at that time, with the exception of Ben-Gurion himself.

When the secret leaked out, *Kol Haam* wrote that "General Harris" had come to Israel "in order to hitch our army to the belligerent chariot of the American imperialists and to look into the conditions for establishing military bases on our country's territory."

The Cold War was raging at full force, but Ben-Gurion was still trying to lead Israel between the raindrops. Israel's first government stated that the country's foreign policy would be based on friendship with all peace-loving nations, "and especially with the United States and the Union of Soviet Socialist Republics." The Soviet Union had supported the establishment of the state, and Communist bloc countries had sold Israel some of its arms during the War of Independence. Thousands of draft-age Jews were allowed to immigrate to Israel from Eastern Europe. There was a large Jewish community in the Soviet Union, and Moscow was the capital of world socialism. Some of the parties in Ben-Gurion's coalition, including his own Mapai party, considered themselves part of the socialist world.

The United States was concerned that Israel would join the Soviet bloc. It therefore established a special fund to disseminate in Israel and several other countries American books, periodicals, films, and records. These cultural items were meant to counterbalance the propaganda that was flowing into Israel from the Soviet Union and its client states. Most Israelis responded enthusiastically to the initiative. Israel also received CARE packages from the United States. The Israeli ability to "get by" rose to the challenge—some of the contents of the CARE packages reached the black market. This was, perhaps, the first manifestation of post-Zionism.

The United States encouraged Israel to integrate into its sphere of influence and in doing so strengthened Mapai. A few days before the first Knesset elections, the American Export-Import Bank decided to grant Israel a $100 million loan to finance immigrant absorption and development projects. It was an almost inconceivable sum at the time. In a letter Ben-Gurion sent to Foreign Minister Moshe Sharett, he wrote that Israel was refraining from joining the Cold War, but ruled that "the State of Israel is not passive or neutral in the world's great debates: in the ideological debate it is democratic and anti-Communist." Moshe Sneh, then a member of Mapam, a left-socialist Zionist and (at the time) Moscow-aligned party, wrote, "Aid is the first station, enslavement the second station, a bloc and bases the third, and from there the way is open to the final station: world war."

When the Korean War broke out, neutrality became nearly impossible for small countries. In the meantime the Soviet Union had abandoned its warm treatment of Israel and was instead trying to develop closer ties with the Arab states. Israel now found itself firmly in the American sphere of influence. Ben-Gurion even toyed with the idea of Israel joining NATO.

One of the first steps toward America took Israel through Germany. The conciliation policy promoted by Ben-Gurion, including the reparations and compensation agreement, involved, as did the choice between the superpowers, a tough moral decision. In the 1950s and early 1960s the Middle East was not high on the American agenda, and Israel at times found itself in conflict with the Americans. Conflicts would occur later as well, but in summing up fifty years of Israel-U.S. relations, Hanan Bar-On, a senior member of Israel's diplomatic service, stated, "Israel's dependence on the United States goes without saying."

. . .

In his 1956 play *I Like Mike*, Aharon Megged satirized what he saw as the Israeli habit of self-abasement before anything coming from America, including the ideal husband for one's daughter. Nevertheless, unlike in several European countries, there was nearly no real public resistance to the penetration of American culture. The Israeli heroism myth had in 1961 already been incarnated in Paul Newman, in the role of Ari Ben Canaan, the hero of the film *Exodus*.

In part, this acceptance was a process of modernization. Israel's first supermarket opened in Tel Aviv in August 1958; in April 1960 the Voice of Israel radio station began its first commercial broadcasts. In the meantime, the first skyscrapers had been erected in Tel Aviv, with a Hilton Hotel opening in one of them. An usher tried to keep the minister of transportation, Moshe Carmel, from entering the hotel's opening ceremony because he had shown up without a tie. A Jewish Agency poster encouraging people to settle in kibbutzim depicted a kibbutz laborer wearing American jeans instead of the classic pioneer khaki or blue work fatigues. The new popular prophet of Israeli urban life was Uri Avneri, the editor of the weekly *Haolam Hazeh*. Avneri covered, and to a large measure invented, a Tel Aviv lifestyle whose symbol was Dizengoff Street and whose heroes were teenagers with Elvis-style greased-back hair. They wore tight pants and pointed shoes, and had a hard time conceiving of anything better than heavy petting in Dad's car.

Avneri was a patriot. He didn't tell his readers that life in the United States was better than life in Israel. He told his readers that living in Israel was good because it could be like living in America. He encouraged this kind of thinking in almost ideological terms. "It is good that this generation has slain the old values and the old concepts," he wrote. "Without destroying the old there is no room for the new." Coca-Cola, Avneri added, was just as good as native Israeli soft drinks and the cha-cha was no less moral than the Krakoviak that the Zionist pioneers had danced. The first bottle of Coca-Cola appeared on the Israeli market in 1968. That same year the country officially began its own television broadcasts.

A series of newspaper ads for Ascot Cigarettes that began to appear in the 1960s were based on photographs of a lifestyle that portrayed the public's American dream: a woman in an evening gown next to a bar with a "USA" poster on the wall behind it, or a muscular young man playing tennis. Like basketball, tennis would later become a salient mark of Americanization. So would the American-accented Hebrew cry, "We're on the map!" shouted by Tal Brody, an American-born Israeli basketball star, when his Maccabi Tel Aviv team won the European Cup. The event was celebrated as a national holiday, even outshining, to a certain extent, the resignation of Prime Minister Yitzhak Rabin that same day. Many Israelis expressed their patriotism through their basketball teams, even when a large proportion of the teams' stars were American acquisitions. Young Israelis were soon sporting American sneakers instead of leather shoes or the traditional sandals.

Once most Israelis lived either in cities or on farms. In the 1980s and 1990s, however, more and more people moved into suburban "bedroom communities," some of which have their own local "country club," mall, and shopping center. People paste up notices on video-rental vending-machines inviting their neighbors to garage sales. The ends of the notices are cut into strips, on each of which is a telephone number, just like in America. People wear ties to work, once considered bourgeois and anti-Zionist, and they commute in their private automobiles. They own more than one car. Road signs are green and blue, as in America. Traffic police wear peaked American caps, emblazoned with the English word *POLICE*.

Many people spend most of their time in front of computers in air-conditioned offices. They receive their mail in long rectangular envelopes instead of the traditional Israeli squat-and-square ones. They send and receive e-mail, do their business on mobile phones, and pay with credit cards, an innovation that caught hold in Israel only in the late 1980s. Prices are often quoted in dollars. Israelis used to have their main meal of the day at lunchtime and follow it with a rest, returning to work in the late afternoon. Now, as in the United States, they eat their dinner in the evening. They are aware of their power as consumers, including their newfound freedom to choose which health plan to belong to and what kind of education their children receive. Some of them hire private security firms to protect their property. The Israeli ideal used to be living on a kibbutz; now it's living in swanky neighborhoods like Tel Aviv's Ramat Aviv Gimmel.

More and more Israelis are aware of the de rigueur of American political correctness. They no longer call people with dark skin *kushim*, after the biblical name for an African kingdom; they call them blacks, just like in the United States. They are aware of issues of environmental quality and the status of women. The law forbids sexual harassment and smoking in public places. Israelis munch hamburgers at McDonald's (one outlet is even kosher), drink milk from cartons instead of the traditional plastic bag, surf bilingual Hebrew-English Web sites. Instead of saying *shalom* when they meet someone and *lehitra'ot* when they part, they say "hi" and "bye." All this reflects a deep change in Israel's identity as a country, in its economy, army, media, and law.

In the mid-1960s the United States began supplying Israel with weaponry. The arms sales increased gradually but steadily. Until then, the Israel Defense Forces had received its most important equipment, including its combat aircraft, from France. The American supplies included Hawk missiles, Patton tanks, and later Skyhawk and Phantom airplanes. In parallel, the army underwent a rapid process of Americanization. "The Israeli Air Force is subject to the inch and the foot," wrote Haifa University's Zvi Sobel. The army's dependence on the United States is so profound, he wrote, "that cutting off the supply line could return Israel to the age of bows and arrows." Historically, this was a transition from the Palmach, the elite force of the Yishuv and War of Independence that operated largely under Soviet inspiration, and the Haganah, the prestate defense force that brought the IDF the British military tradition. U.S. scientists and philanthropists also helped Israel develop its nuclear capability.

In 1968 Israel sent a new ambassador to the United States: Yitzhak Rabin, who had been the army's chief of staff during the Six Day War. Rabin, whose father had come to Palestine from Russia via the United States, was among those Israelis who fostered and even symbolized the American dream. "I view the tightening of the connection to the United States and the strengthening of strategic defense between it and Israel as our greatest challenge. . . . The diplomatic struggle will be focused in Washington. It is there that Israel's war for its future will continue," he wrote.

Ambassador Rabin's tenure in Washington coincided with the terms of Richard Nixon and Henry Kissinger, during which the United States became ever more willing to supply Israel with military aid. During the 1973 Yom Kippur War, Nixon asked Congress to approve aid to Israel in the amount of $2.2 billion. The airlift from the United States included a variety of equipment and ammunition, including air-to-air and air-to-ground missiles, artillery, armaments for combat planes, tanks, radios, and other weaponry for a total worth of more than $800 million. As part of its growing relationship with the U.S. military, the IDF adopted organizational and combat doctrines based on American practices. Israeli officers went to the United States for courses, and before long a phenomenon appeared in the IDF that would soon characterize Israeli society as a whole. Rabin was one of its personifications. Israel's elites, in all areas, began to be filled by people who received their training in the United States. Many of them saw America as an ideal.

In its early years, when Israel was still ruled by the labor movement, the government's economic policy was aimed at promoting national goals, first and foremost strong defense and immigrant absorption. It was an economy mobilized in the state interest, in the spirit of the socialist and social-democratic ideology that the labor movement represented. Economic policy was also used to reinforce the dominance of the parties of the labor movement, and in particular Mapai, the largest. The Histadrut, the national labor federation that was controlled by Mapai, also played a central role. The state was the major power directing the principal social and economic processes, the most important of which was the absorption of more than one million immigrants, most of them indigent. Many came from underdeveloped countries and had not been prepared for life in a modern society. Many did not even know how to read and write. In those years, Israelis were supposed to think and feel in the first person plural. The national social, political, and ideological elite was a relatively small group, many of whom lived in kibbutzim.

Yet Israel's economic story proceeded, almost without reversals, in the direction of privatization and private enterprise. The process was gradual, but its most dramatic milestone came in May 1977, when Mapai, now the Labor Party, lost its first election and the opposition Likud came into power. The new minister of finance, Simcha Erlich, was the leader of the free-market Liberal Party, one of the Likud's constituent factions. An early guest of the government was Milton Friedman, America's high priest of the free market. Not coincidentally, the new prime minister, Menachem Begin, singled out the kibbutzim as a target for attack. The social, economic, and ideological metamorphosis that accompanied the decline of the kibbutzim symbolized the transition from an explicit commitment to socialist values to the age of the free market.

In time the Histadrut also lost its economic power; the income gap between rich and poor grew larger. All this took place as Israel became increasingly dependent on economic aid from the United States. This dependence made it much like the old, pre-Zionist Jewish community in the Holy Land, which also lived off charity, primarily from Jews in the United States. Israel's economic history is thus a classically Jewish story, far from the ideal conceived by some of the founders of the Zionist movement.

Nixon's and Kissinger's America was still very much an ideological country, engaged in the Cold War and Vietnam. Israel itself was in the midst of its own ideological awakening brought on by the Six Day War. But in the United States a series of revolutions in values entirely changed society, making it more egalitarian, and human and civil rights were strengthened. After the Six Day War, however, it seemed as if the spirit of the 1960s were passing over Israel. In fact, it simply came late. When it arrived, it changed Israeli society in the same way in which America had changed.

The protest against American involvement in Vietnam was incarnated in Israel as protest against Israel's occupation of the territories conquered in 1967. The American civil rights struggle became, in Israel, the fight against discrimination of Sephardic Jews, those whose families came from the Islamic world. Some young members of the Sephardic community founded an organization called the Black Panthers. Some of the young people who founded Peace Now in the 1970s were American-born; others had studied at American universities. In establishing an Israeli peace movement, they were imitating the American peace movement, and with it they copied an entire culture.

This American spirit, which produced the Camp David agreements between Israel and Egypt, would later lead people to feel they had had enough of the occupation of the West Bank and Gaza Strip. It also produced Israel's unilateral withdrawal from Lebanon in 2000. The peace agreements with Egypt and Jordan and the agreements between Israel and the Palestinians were all signed under the sponsorship of the United States and due to the intense personal involvement of the sitting president. All these agreements were made possible, to a large extent, because of the willingness of the American people to finance them. They also reflect Israel's dependence on the U. S., and the depth of American penetration of all areas of Israeli life.

The choice of Senator Joseph Lieberman as the Democratic Party's candidate for vice president in 2000 played out in the local media almost as if it were Israeli news. David Landau of *Ha'aretz* described the choice as "an amazing and stunning event" and expressed his hope that Israel might achieve a similar level of liberality and political maturity. "May we hope that the choice of Lieberman—an important milestone in American history and a huge event in the history of the Jewish people—be for us Israelis, despite all the differences between here and there, a cause for introspection and perhaps even inspiration?"

As in America, Israeli politics has become more personal and more commercialized; candidates for prime minister now debate in the spirit of the debates broadcast on American television. This political style received formal expression when the system was changed, for a time, to provide for direct election of the prime minister. The rise of Benjamin Netanyahu in the 1990s was an important step in the Americanization of Israeli politics. Netanyahu came of age in the United States; Washington, D.C., is the capital of his inner world.

His accession to power also symbolized a change in attitude toward Israelis who had emigrated to the United States. Rabin had once berated the emigrants as "gutless scum." Yet, as the years went by, there was hardly an Israeli family without an emigrant, generally in America. In the 1980s Israel's television station broadcast a commercial aimed at encouraging people to make overseas phone calls to the United States. Such a message could hardly have been imagined just a few years before, not only because people were expected to be ashamed of their expatriate family members, but also because many people didn't have telephones. They waited years to get one, and the government, which had a monopoly on telephone services, had no interest in urging people to call overseas. The telephone network was later transferred to a government corporation, Bezek, as part of a policy of shifting responsibility for the provision of public services from the government to commercial enterprises. Just like America.

The TV commercial depicted an elderly couple calling their son, daughter-in-law, and grandchildren in the United States. The situation is crystal-clear—the family living overseas is not there temporarily. They are not tourists, students, or Jewish Agency emissaries sent to encourage immigration to Israel. America is their home. In an instant, living in the United States became legitimate and unremarkable. These days, insurance companies offer special policies for "Israelis in America." Newspapers print ads that tell Israelis how to participate in the worldwide green card lottery. Granting legitimacy to living abroad followed on the heels of granting legitimacy to Jewish life outside Israel. Both changes reflect a coming to terms with non-Zionist, or at least non-Israeli, Jewish alternatives.

Most Israelis see the September 11, 2001 attack on New York as an attack on Tel Aviv, identifying their own war on terrorism with America's. At the same time, they perceive America as a refuge, permanent or temporary, from the sweaty, arduous task of being Israeli. "When they start shooting I start missing New York," wrote Sami Shalom Shitrit after one of the waves of violence between the Israeli army and the Palestinians.

> It began on a hill in Lebanon, even before that shitty war. Everyone was shooting like lunatics and Shemesh the sergeant called me over. He took out a U.S. road map and started describing the coast-to-coast motorcycle trip we'd do together right after our discharge. That's what gave him strength in the face of all that helplessness and madness. Afterward, we spent months learning the route from New York to Los Angeles, with a big zigzag from north to south. It was the greatest trek of my life, made in the dark, with a flashlight, on the laminated road map.

More than any previous politician, Benjamin Netanyahu based his career on his television appearances. In this, his election symbolized not only the Americanization of politics but also of the Israeli media. Television broadcasts gave the United States much greater influence in Israel, as elsewhere in the world. Most of the programs broadcast are imported from the United States, and nearly all of them are influenced by it. As a result of TV, people changed their daily schedules; they began to dress differently, eat differently, enjoy themselves differently, speak differently, think differently, and feel differently. For a time television had a unifying influence—everyone spoke about what they had seen the previous night. People became more involved in politics and social problems. But television also made Israelis much more aware of themselves as individuals. They began to discover themselves as individuals distinct from the national collective, and as members of local communities with their own identities. In providing this new frame of reference, television contributed to the second notable innovation that Americanization brought the Israeli media: the local newspaper.

The ideological party-sponsored dailies abundant in the prestate period and Israel's early years closed one after another in the 1970s and 1980s. They were replaced by publications addressing issues previously unfamiliar to most Israelis, such as environmental quality, consumerism, and the local leisure culture. At around the same time a new style appeared, unacceptable in the Israeli press of the past. New journalism was a direct import from the United States via writers who had spent time there. They brought back concepts, expressions, and even entire grammatical structures that existed only in English. When they returned, these new journalists joined a new echelon of leaders in almost every area. An American chapter was usual, almost mandatory, in the biographies of the Israeli elite.

The new journalism claimed to present the reader with the "real story" or the "story behind the story." The emphasis was on individuals, including the journalist himself, not entire societies, not ideas, not processes. What had once been considered an elitist propensity was then adopted as a guideline for the media as a whole. More and more personal stories, many of them not political, took the place of political news. The trend became even more profound when television began to offer multiple channels. Local stations appeared alongside local newspapers. Locality was, apparently, the most decisive American influence on the public—they were now individuals. They stopped being first person plural. They were I's. Private radio stations and Internet sites led to increasing individualism in the media. The process was also reflected in Hebrew fiction, poetry, and popular culture.

Israel's new individualistic awareness was a real revolution. It encouraged equality between the sexes and sexual permissiveness, and gave a measure of legitimacy to unconventional sexual orientations. Military service, and service as a combat officer in particular, changed in the perception of many from a contribution to society to the first station on the road to joining the elite. Many young Israelis began to think of their post-discharge trip to India as the climax of their military service—an escape from every restraining framework, a return to liberated childhood. The number of men and women who do not serve in the army is steadily rising. Sami Shalom Shitrit wrote of this trend:

> These kids have received something that previous generations did not have—citizenship of the world. Thanks to satellite, cable television, and electronic communication the world has entered the home of almost every boy and girl. And they have developed a sense of belonging to large swathes of our global

community. The boundaries between states are losing their significance, so the need to get killed over them becomes illogical to these kids, citizens of the world.

It's worth keeping this development in mind, because its momentum will only increase in the next century. It's worth thinking about more significant compensation for military service, beyond sense of mission and pride in the unit. I'm speaking about real wages, about true professional challenges, about free higher education, about lots of veteran benefits, and so on. There's no escaping it. Classes in Jewish and Israeli heritage won't lead people to sacrifice themselves. Even fundamentalist suicide bombers do what they do for personal benefit in the next world.

The willingness to accept individual discretion in whether or not to serve in the army extended to providing an official seal of approval to practices that had once been tacitly tolerated but never accepted. A case in point: ultra-Orthodox yeshiva students were exempted from military service under an agreement Ben-Gurion had reached with the Agudat Yisrael party when the state was founded. The exemption was incorporated into military regulations but never legislated; Israeli law continued to mandate universal service.

Initially, the exemption applied to a handful of young men each year. But in the 1980s and 1990s, as the ultra-Orthodox population grew, the number of exemptions increased to thousands each year. Those Israelis who did serve began to protest the inequity of the arrangement. A government commission set up to study the issue responded with a proposal to codify this evasion of service into law; in other words, what had once been a tolerated anomaly in the principle of universal military service was to be accepted formally by the public's representatives in the Knesset.

At some point even war, that fundamental collective Israeli experience, underwent a kind of privatization. Arab terrorism did not threaten the country's existence. Instead, it endangered the personal security of each individual. This is true of the Gulf War as well. Everyone knew that the missiles Iraq fired at Israel were no danger to the country itself. They did, however, threaten the lives of individuals.

The Gulf War was a distinctly individual experience. People sat in their sealed rooms, isolated from their neighbors, with gas masks on their faces that isolated them from their families as well. They followed the war on CNN, whose reception in Israel was itself one stage in the Americanization process. There were several minutes of tension—will the missile hit me or not? Large numbers of Israelis left their homes, especially in Tel Aviv, and went to stay in safer places. In a number of cases, this prevented disaster; some of the homes hit by missiles had been vacated by fleeing families.

Running away from the SCUDs was controversial. Some demanded a more steadfast, patriotic stand. The flight of the Tel Aviv elite in the Gulf War was a precedent that later legitimized flight from Kiryat Shemona, near the Lebanese border. In the past, when the town was a favorite target for Palestinian rockets, its residents descended to their bomb shelters and sweated out the attack. Politicians and the media expressed compassion for their suffering and extolled their bravery. In the 1990s, under attack from the Shiite Hezbollah militia, many of the town's residents packed their bags and headed south and no one thought to criticize them.

In parallel, there was also a "judicial revolution," whose most important element was protection of civil rights and of some human rights, in the spirit of the American constitution.

It is hard to exaggerate the importance of the Supreme Court's influence on public life in Israel. Likewise, it is hard to exaggerate the influence of the U.S. Constitution on the Supreme Court's rulings. Its influence has grown over the years and has become even more profound under the tenure of Aharon Barak, the current chief justice. Barak was an active partner in drafting a series of Basic Laws, which together constitute a kind of Israeli constitution. One of these is the Basic Law: Human Dignity and Liberty.

The court's activism has largely been in the area of civil rights for Jews. Its rulings on civil rights for Arabs, be they Israeli citizens or residents of the occupied territories, is less impressive. The court has, for example, sanctioned some of the injustices of the military government that were imposed on Israel's Arab citizens until the mid-1960s and on the West

Bank and Gaza Strip after the Six Day War. It has, time and again, upheld deportations, house demolitions, and even torture.

It is against this background that the Supreme Court's recent ruling in the case of 'Adel and Iman Qa'adan stands out, one of the most revolutionary rulings in the country's history, as Chief Justice Barak was well aware at the time. "We are today taking a first step along an arduous and sensitive road," he wrote. "Let us rather advance cautiously from case to case, according to the circumstances of each one. Yet, even if the road is long, it is important for us to keep our eyes not on where we came from but where we are heading."

'Adel Qa'adan, a nurse at Hillel Yaffe Hospital in the town of Hadera, and his wife, Iman, a teacher, have two children and come from an Arab village in Israel, Baka al-Gharbiyya. They looked into the possibility of purchasing a home in a new settlement, Katzir, being built by the Jewish Agency on land it received for this purpose from the state. Katzir lies not far from Afula, a small city in the Jezre'el Valley to the east of Hadera. The site was originally occupied by the army, which prepared it for civilian settlement, and then became a kibbutz that belonged to the left-wing Hashomer Hatzair movement. The site was later given to a cooperative association that wanted to set up a "communal settlement," a type of small village that generally serves as a bedroom suburb where middle-class families live in rural surroundings while commuting to jobs in nearby urban centers. Communal settlements are governed by the associations that set them up, and these have the legal power to select which families will be allowed to build homes in the village.

The cooperative association informed the Qa'adans that they would not be allowed to build a house in the settlement because they are Arabs and the village is designated for Jews alone. The Qa'adans petitioned the Supreme Court.

The decision to bring the question before the court was itself an innovation. In Zionism's hundred years, hundreds of settlements designated for Jews alone had been established throughout the country. Arabs cannot live in them. The Association for Civil Rights in Israel, which represented the family, was aware of the issue's sensitive nature and took care to emphasize that it was not seeking to challenge Zionist history: "The petitioners are not focusing their arguments on the legitimacy of the policy that prevailed in this matter during the period that preceded the establishment of the state and in the years that have passed since its establishment. Nor are they challenging the decisive role played by the Jewish Agency in settling Jews throughout the land during the course of this century."

The Jewish Agency argued that Katzir was one link in a chain of small settlements that were meant to preserve Israel's open spaces for the Jewish people, and that its establishment promotes the goal of settling Jews throughout the country, and in particular in areas that are sparsely inhabited by Jews. They also cited the need to disperse the population across Israel for security reasons. The cooperative association argued that Arab residents of the village would have difficulty performing guard duty, incumbent on all the families since the settlement had been the target of terrorist attacks. Furthermore, it claimed, the presence of Arabs would be liable to lead Jewish families to leave the settlement, turning it in the end from a Jewish into an Arab village. Also, not far away, in a settlement called Charish, Arabs were in fact allowed to build houses.

This was a classically American dilemma, and Barak read American court decisions in the process of preparing his ruling. One of these was the U.S. Supreme Court's famous 1954 ruling in *Brown v. Board of Education*. That case addressed the practice of maintaining separate schools for whites and "Afro-Americans," Barak explained in his opinion, as if the semantics of American political correctness had to be observed in Hebrew as well. He also quoted American court rulings that deal with the complex nature of equality, including the question of whether separate but equal facilities can be established for whites and blacks, or in the Israeli instance between Jews and Arabs—schools in the American case, settlements in the Israeli case. The U.S. Supreme Court held that separate is inherently unequal. Barak ruled that there are circumstances in which separate but equal is legal, for example so as to refrain from imposing assimilation on a minority group seeking to preserve its separate status.

Ever so cautiously, taking care not to undermine the Zionist foundations of the state, Chief Justice Barak stated that his ruling was directed toward the future, instructing the Jewish

Agency to "reconsider" the plaintiffs' request, this time on the basis of the principle of equality. The key point of the ruling was that the equality ought to guide the state's activities since it is, according to the Basic Law: Human Dignity and Liberty, both "Jewish and democratic." Four of the five judges sitting on the case concurred. Prior to the ruling, Barak asked the parties to reach an accommodation that would make it possible to avoid a ruling, but when they did not do so he said he faced one of the most difficult decisions of his life.

While Barak was laboring on his opinion, Member of Knesset Amnon Rubinstein published an article in *Ha'aretz* in which he called for the nationalization of the land belonging to the Jewish National Fund (JNF), the land purchase and management organization, one of Zionism's founding institutions. The JNF's chairman responded: "Mr. Rubinstein's article serves those who seek to sever, break, and shatter the connection between the Jewish people and their homeland and so to accelerate the process of changing the State of Israel's character and nature from a state of the Jewish people to a state of all its citizens, devoid of a Jewish soul and spirit."

The JNF chairman did not evade the issue of equality. "[It] is a fundamental value in the life of the Jewish people's state, precisely because the state is Jewish, and everything must be done to internalize equality as a value in our life as an independent nation," he wrote, volunteering, in the name of his organization, to free Israel from the need to act in contradiction of the principle of equality. "Entrusting the Jewish people's land to the JNF frees the State of Israel, even though it is the state of the Jewish people, from having to deal with this issue and in so doing to violate the principle of equality."

Chief Justice Barak seems to have feared that his ruling would be interpreted as a retreat from the definition of Israel as a Jewish state. "The State of Israel's values as . . . Jewish and democratic," he wrote, "are based, among other things, on the right of the Jewish people to stand independent in its sovereign country." And indeed, "the Jewish people's return to its homeland is a consequence of Israel's values as both a Jewish and a democratic state." This sentence was apparently formulated to justify the Law of Return that grants citizenship to Jews immediately upon their arrival in Israel. "It is thus obvious that Hebrew will be the country's principal language and that its principal holidays will reflect the national revival of the Jewish people; it is also obvious that Jewish heritage will be the central element in the state's national and cultural heritage." To remove all doubt, Barak also devoted several lines to the Jewish Agency's role in realizing the Zionist vision, the ingathering of the exiles, and in making the country fertile and productive. He noted generously that the Jewish Agency had not yet completed the mission assigned to it. According to Barak, "There is no contradiction between the values of the State of Israel as a Jewish and democratic state and complete equality among its citizens. On the contrary, equal rights for all people in Israel, whatever their religion and whatever their nationality, derives from the values of the State of Israel as a Jewish and democratic state."

The Supreme Court's attempt to pull the punch aimed at one of the pillars of Zionism in the Land of Israel was only partially successful. Some Israelis reacted heatedly to the ruling; the Likud faction in the Knesset issued a statement saying that the court's decision heralded the end of Israel as a Jewish state. This might happen, the statement declared, even if "perhaps" the justices had intended no such a thing.

Of course they had intended no such thing. The faith that it is possible to combine the fundamental principles of democracy with the state's Jewish character is not entirely unfounded. But keeping the state Jewish and democratic is not as difficult as keeping it Zionist and democratic. This is a classic post-Zionist conundrum.

Apart from its effect on Israeli Zionism, there are indications that America has also influenced the religious identity of some Israelis. At the beginning of 2000 the Movement for Progressive Judaism, Reform Judaism's organization in Israel, published a survey purportedly showing that 35 percent of the Jewish population identified with Reform practices current for the most part in the United States. In fact, most of those who claim to "identify" with Reform Judaism define themselves as nonreligious. A survey sponsored by an American ultra-Orthodox group produced results that seem more in line with reality. From whom, Israelis were asked, would they prefer to receive religious services, such as circumcision, marriage, and funerals? A total of 22.3 percent said they would like to have these ceremonies conducted by the Reform movement. Just like in America.

···

FACING
OVADIA'S STATUE

···

"The Real Zionists Are Us"

The souvenir shop at the Judaica Center in Gush Etzion specializes in art objects and Jewish ritual items. At the beginning of 2000 it offered for sale a miniature statue, about eighteen inches high, of Rabbi Ovadia Yosef, with a $1,000 price tag. The papier-mâché image depicts the rabbi dressed in the purple robe and cloth hat that are the traditional garments of the spiritual leader of Israel's Sephardic Jewish community. His face is stern, as befits his position.

The salesladies in the shop speak English; Rabbi Yosef is popular in America as well. His staff employs the most modern communications technologies, just like fundamentalist preachers in the United States. Rabbi Yosef's weekly Torah lesson is broadcast by satellite from one end of the world to the other. He has a large Web site where, for a price quoted in dollars, people can pay for the rabbi to mention them by name in a blessing. Videotapes of Rabbi Yosef are available. There is also a service that will place a note bearing people's personal prayers and supplications between the stones of the Western Wall for them without actually having to go there themselves—the prayers can be sent by fax. Some conclude from this that Judaism is adjusting itself to modern life. In fact, modern Israel is continually becoming more Jewish. This is the main reason why the conflict between religious and non-religious Israelis, a central arena of the local culture wars, has not yet led to full-scale civil hostilities.

A few months after the British conquered Palestine, the Zionist movement made an attempt to buy the Western Wall from its Arab owners. At the same time, the first preparations were being made for the establishment of the Hebrew University. The purchase of the Western Wall was meant to end the ultra-Orthodox monopoly on Judaism, while the Hebrew University was often referred to as a Zionist temple.

At that time it seemed as if the Yishuv, the new Jewish community in Palestine that emerged as a result of Zionist immigration, was creating a secular, "post-Jewish" society. Yudke, the hero of Haim Hazaz's story "Sermon," believed that Judaism and Zionism were contradictory. "When a man can't be Jewish he becomes a Zionist," Yudke declared. "This is no exaggeration. . . . Zionism begins at the point of Judaism's destruction, from the point where the people's strength has been exhausted. That's a fact!"

To strive for economic, social, political, and military

normalization—to return to cultivation of the land and other productive trades, achieve independence, and establish a defense force—is not inevitably to be secular, according to Uriel Simon, a religious Zionist thinker. But normalization in all these spheres has involved, and even been conditioned on, spiritual-cultural normalization, meaning a give-and-take relationship with international culture. In this the Zionist movement adopted the values and aspirations of the Jewish Enlightenment. Devotion to sacred studies to the exclusion of all else was seen as an obstacle to national revival.

Liberal values attracted the Zionists because of their liberating power, and because they were perceived as a necessary condition for the development of science and technology, for the establishment of a democratic system of government, and for the advancement of literature and art. Without these values the Jewish people would not be able to break out of the ghetto into the wide-open spaces of their homeland. This is the revolutionary element in Zionist ideology. Simon has identified another element: romanticism.

Among "the follies of the romantic spirit" that characterized Zionist ideology, Simon cited unswerving devotion to the Land of Israel and the rejection of Uganda as an alternative; the enormous efforts put into reviving the Hebrew language; and intensive study of the Bible, the foundation stone of the renewed national culture. Non-religious Zionists insisted on being married in accordance with Jewish religious law, circumcising their sons, fasting on Yom Kippur, and celebrating at least some of the Jewish holidays, as if these religious precepts were part of a unique and unifying national way of life.

On top of all these practices was a secular incarnation of the religious belief that the Jews were a chosen people. This was expressed, for example, in a tendency to view the kibbutz as a real contribution to the creation of a better world, alongside an explicit national commitment to equality, the "purity of arms," and other values. These ethical principles were seen as being incumbent on Israel precisely because it was a Jewish state, and some of them were even enacted into law. The intention was to intensify the state's Jewish character without giving in to pressures from religious and ultra-Orthodox circles to institute traditional Jewish law as the country's legal system. Purchase of the Western Wall by the Zionist quasi-government of the Yishuv was meant to turn the site from a religious to a national symbol; the establishment of the Hebrew University on Mount Scopus, overlooking the Temple Mount, was meant to mark secular knowledge, rather than religious practice, as the focal point of the new Jewish commonwealth. There were even attempts to impose the new nationalism on the religious population. Soon after the establishment of the British Mandate, Chaim Weizmann tried to condition the distribution of aid to Jerusalem's ultra-Orthodox Jews, many of whom were on the brink of starvation, on their replacing Yiddish with Hebrew as the language of instruction in their yeshivas.

The ultra-Orthodox community, called the Old Yishuv, became a minority and, at the time of the state's establishment, feared that its way of life would become untenable. The attempt to preserve that way of life was not, generally, an ideological struggle. It was, from the ultra-Orthodox point of view, a battle for their very existence. While in Israel today the term *religious coercion* invariably refers to ultra-Orthodox attempts to impose religious observance on the secular population, at the time of independence it had the opposite connotation. Then it was used to refer to the possibility that the state might force ultra-Orthodox Jews to live in a way that violated their religious conscience. The state, they feared, would force them to send their children to non-religious schools, their women to serve in the army, and allow mixed marriages between Jews and non-Jews. Shortly before the War of Independence, Amram Blau, the leader of Ha'eda Ha'haredit, an extreme anti-Zionist ultra-Orthodox group in Jerusalem, declared that his community would surrender to the Arabs without a fight and unconditionally, and asked that he and his followers be issued United Nations passports.

The more numerous section of the Orthodox community represented by the Agudat Yisrael party was also anti-Zionist and concerned about the consequences of becoming citizens of a secular Zionist state. However, being more pragmatic, they entered into negotiations with the leaders of the state-in-waiting. This resulted in their receipt of a letter from Jewish Agency chairman David Ben-Gurion and two other top Agency officials, that promised the state would not encroach on the religious conscience of its citizens. The weekly day of rest would be the Jewish Sabbath; state-sponsored kitchens in schools and the army would be kosher. A somewhat vague part of the letter promised that the state would not institute civil marriage, and a more explicit section promised the autonomy of the religious school system.

This was the foundation of the religious "status quo" in a state that was supposed to have been secular. The Declaration of Independence defined Israel as a Jewish state but justified its establishment with historical arguments, not religious ones. God was not supposed to appear in the Declaration. After a protracted fight, however, the religious Zionists succeeded in inserting the pseudonymous "Rock of Israel" in the final paragraph.

The attempt to give the state a secular character led to a series of struggles that began immediately after independence. In the 1950s and 1960s it often seemed as if the fissure between the secular and religious communities would lead to civil war. "Against the flexed God-wrathfulness of Neturei Karta [the most extreme of the ultra-Orthodox groups] a second camp, no less zealous, stands and organizes itself, one of aggressive atheists," declared Knesset Member Ari Jabotinsky, son of Ze'ev Jabotinsky, whose Revisionist Zionists were the forebears of today's Likud party. Jabotinsky once protested against his inability to obtain a ham sandwich in the Knesset cafeteria. In defending secular education, Knesset Member Devorah Netzer of Mapai declared, "This is our religion, in this we believe." The religious-secular split made it impossible to draft a constitution for the new country.

The Zionist state found it difficult to influence ultra-Orthodox schools, but it tried to take charge of educating the children of new immigrants. Many of the new immigrants lived in accordance with religious tradition and law, including most of the Yemenite community that had arrived en masse after independence. "The common foundation," wrote one of the officials in charge of formulating the educational program for these children, "is the spiritual strength that has been created here for the most part or perhaps only by the labor movement, and which today belongs to all and to the state."

The only Jewish element in the curriculum was the study of the Bible, which was "to be presented in terms of the Israeli elements that interest us today. . . . The narrative and the descriptions are to be turned into a living depiction of the Israeli's life in his land." According to the official who supervised education in the immigrant camps: "We have liberated the biblical verses of their ornateness and we have given them back their fundamental, true meaning," he wrote. " 'Six days shalt thou labor,' 'And thou shalt love,' 'justice shalt thou pursue,' 'proclaim liberty throughout the land and to all the inhabitants thereof'—all these are the foundations of a worldview that we have tried to apply in our working settlements in particular and in the labor movement as a whole." The attempt to impose a uniform secular education on the entire population failed. Both the state religious school system, run according to religious Zionists principles, and the ultra-Orthodox school system survived and even grew.

• • •

In November 1957 a boy named Aharon Steinberg died in the village of Pardes Hanna. His mother was not Jewish, so the boy was buried not in the main part of the local cemetery, but "outside the fence." A public scandal ensued, in the wake of which the minister of interior, Yisrael Bar-Yehuda, ordered that new immigrants should be registered as Jews upon their own declaration, unless it was possible to prove otherwise. The minister's order produced an even stormier debate. The religious parties demanded that the official rabbinate be the sole judge of a person's Jewish status, in accordance with the general rule that "the State of Israel will consider Jewish anyone who is considered Jewish according to the laws of the Torah." The parties of the left demanded, in turn, that the state cease altogether to register the ethnic affiliation and religion of its inhabitants.

As the controversy grew ever more heated, Prime Minister David Ben-Gurion wrote to several dozen "wise Jews"—rabbis, thinkers, and writers—and asked their opinion on the question of "who is a Jew." His very willingness to hear the opinions of non-Zionist rabbis, some of whom did not even live in Israel, was a concession on his part, as if Israel were recognizing that Jews living overseas had a right to intervene in internal affairs. Throughout the years the Supreme Court was petitioned over and over again to rule on who is a Jew. The question has continued to weigh on the Israeli public and has remained without any consensual solution. The present legal situation is that in matters of personal status, such as marriage and divorce, Jewish affiliation is awarded only to people with Jewish mothers, or to those who have been converted to Judaism by an Orthodox rabbinical court. To receive Israeli citizenship under the Law of Return, it is sufficient to have one Jewish grandparent: such citizens may bring non-Jewish relatives into the country.

The conflict over religion's place in the state has been resolved for the most part through practical compromises of one sort or another, by means of political negotiations. All these arrangements indicate that Israeli culture has not succeeded in formulating a relevant alternative to Jewish culture. In the 1930s most kibbutzim did away with observance of the Sabbath and the dietary laws, and in some cases religious marriage and burial as well. Here and there they tried to design secular alternatives to holiday ceremonies and even composed secular texts to recite on these occasions. The kibbutz movement published a secular Hagadah.

These alternatives did not, however, produce a real secular culture. Uriel Simon wrote: "The important and lasting achievements of 200 years of secular Jewish creativity in the spirit of the Enlightenment are not a sufficient foundation for constructing an Israeli national-cultural identity. Furthermore, these achievements themselves stand on the shoulders of 3,000 years of creativity that is principally religious in nature." The common Jewish foundation that is shared by most of Israel's citizens, including those who are not religious, has prevented the tension from degenerating into an absolute break. At the bottom line, at the last minute, they have always said, "After all, we're all Jews."

In the country's early years, Israelis had to confront the fact that the establishment of the state did not bring about the hoped-for normalization of relations between the Jewish people and other nations. "In direct contradiction to the Zionist thesis," Simon wrote, "according to which antisemitism was primarily the result of the abnormal status of Diaspora Jews, antisemitism returned and grew, reincarnated as condemnation of Zionism and animosity toward Israel." This disappointment formed the basis for Zionist doubt. But then came the great victory of the Six Day War.

The conquest of the Western Wall, the Tomb of the Patriarchs in Hebron, and other holy sites gave a huge impetus to the Jewish component of Israeli identity. Until then, the Israeli army held swearing-in ceremonies for new recruits at Masada, the heroic Hebrew stronghold; since the Six Day War such ceremonies have been conducted at the Western Wall. This symbolized abandonment of the concept of the army as a small band of resolute fighters defending the nation against a strong and numerous enemy. Israeli military power began to be seen by many as an instrument of messianic theology.

The settlers of the West Bank and Gaza Strip became the new pioneers, and the knitted yarmulka, the modern incarnation of the traditional male head covering, became the badge of the religious Zionists; it replaced the cloth hat, the symbol of pioneering labor Zionist Israel. The Gush Emunim movement, which promoted Israeli settlement in the occupied territories, claimed a monopoly on patriotism, and messianic sanctity was ascribed to the state itself. Gush Emunim's spiritual leader, Rabbi Tzvi Yehuda Kook, wrote:

> There is one general principal thing: the state. It is entirely holy and there is no flaw in it. It is a sublime heavenly incarnation of 'He who returns His divine presence to Zion.' All the rest is details, trifles, problems, and complications; there is nothing in them that can mar, in any way whatsoever, the full force of the state's sanctity. The intrinsic value of the state does not depend on whether it contains more or fewer observers of the Torah and its commandments. Certainly, the aspiration is that the entire nation 'belong' to the Torah and the commandments, but the state is holy in any and every case.

Messianic patriotism identified itself as true Zionism, but in fact it dragged the state into a manifestly post-Zionist reality. The settlements in the occupied territories constitute a Jewish minority within a non-Jewish majority population, in violation of the principle guiding the Zionist movement since the inception of its activity in the Land of Israel: a large Jewish majority, even in part of the land, had always been preferable to holding on to areas populated by Arabs. The notion of separation between Jews and Palestinian Arabs is today attributed to Yitzhak Rabin and Ehud Barak, but was almost certainly the principle that guided Ben-Gurion when he decided during the War of Independence not to conquer the West Bank and opposed its conquest during the Six Day War. After the war he declared that it was better to have peace in a small Israel than war in Greater Israel. The settlers' willingness to live as a Jewish minority within a non-Jewish majority links them, paradoxically, to the tradition of Jewish life in the Exile.

The awakening prompted by the Six Day War attracted large numbers of young Jews from the United States, some of them followers of Rabbi Meir Kahane. An American import, Kahane was an extreme religious nationalist and power guru who specialized in inflaming crowds with incendiary racist rhetoric. Israel also experienced a wave of return to religion, a fashion that reached the middle class as well. On Lag B'Omer, in the spring, Israelis flocked to the mystical celebration of Talmudic rabbi Shimon Bar Yochai at Mount Meron in the Galilee. The Hasidic Klezmer music festival held in Safed turned from an esoteric event for aficionados to a cultural institution.

In 1980 the Knesset revoked a legislative provision requiring courts to rule in accordance with English common law and rules of equity when Israeli law provided no guidance. Instead, judges were referred to the principles of justice, honesty, and peace in the "Hebrew law." This section in the Foundations of Law ruling led to disagreements among the justices of the Supreme Court on how it should be applied. Like a series of other events, this was a road sign on Israel's journey toward Judaism. People whose families had Hebraicized their names when they immigrated to Israel began returning to the original Yiddish and Arabic; universities and even high schools began offering courses in Yiddish. The Ministry of Education decided that immigrant students could take part of their graduation exams in Russian or Amharic, a deviation from the enforcement of Hebrew exclusivity that would have been unthinkable a generation ago. Yoram Kaniuk, a Palmach veteran who flirted in the past with Canaanite ideology and even changed his name under its influence, wrote in 2000, "I feel I am first a Jew and only afterward an Israeli." In the meantime he had reverted to his original name.

One day in 1965, after the weeklong Passover holiday, some three hundred people gathered in the Herzl Forest near the city of Lod for a picnic that made history. Many of the picnickers came from Yad Rambam, a nearby semicollective farming village populated for the most part by immigrants from the city of Fez in Morocco, where the rabbi and philosopher Maimonides once lived. One of the participants, Shaul Ben-Simhon of Ashdod, previously of Fez, was a member of the Histadrut's central committee.

Not long before, several members of nearby farming villages had come to him to ask for help. Most of them were unemployed. Ben-Simchon could do nothing to solve their problem, but he accepted an idea suggested by one of the men: reviving the Mimouna, a celebration long observed by the Jews of Morocco on the day following Passover.

Most Jews who immigrated to Israel during the country's first years came from Arab countries. The vast majority did not want to give up their traditions. Compelled to adopt new ways of life, they retained religious tradition as a dominant part of their identities. Immigrants from Europe had already adopted secular Jewish lifestyles, but they also brought with them elements of a traditional identity that grew in part out of the discrimination and persecution suffered as Jews during the Holocaust or afterward in the Communist bloc. Few of these newcomers wanted a new Israeli identity, and among those who did, few succeeded in fashioning one. Even if they took Hebrew names, they were unable to change themselves.

No one really knows the true origins of the Mimouna. A cash prize was even on offer at one time to anyone who could figure it out. There are those who associate it with the anniversary of the death of Rabbi Maimon ben Yosef, Maimonides' father, or with Maimonides himself. In any event, in Morocco the day was a kind of communal open house, involving visits to families, friends, and neighbors and the consumption of traditional foods. In Israel, however, the revived Mimouna was celebrated with huge communal picnics in public parks.

The holiday spread throughout Israel and grew by the year. Hundreds of thousands of Jews of Moroccan origin participated. Government officials and political leaders stopped by; as one of the largest Israeli ethnic communities, the Moroccan constituency had to be cultivated by any candidate aspiring to local or national office. A few years after the public celebration was instituted, a labor contract was signed with Ashdod's longshoremen that contained a provision allowing them to take a day off for the holiday. It soon became an optional day off for all public sector employees. Some viewed the Mimouna's institutionalization as a deliberate establishment ploy to blunt the social and political consciousness of the Sephardic Jewish population. The costs of the celebration were indeed paid in large part out of municipal and national government coffers. In fact, a long series of attempts to rouse the community to protest poverty and discrimination failed. This was true both when the protest was revolutionary and violent and when it took place within the normal political process.

The Mimouna festivities became institutionalized, and the presence of senior politicians gave them an official flavor. In a sense, they redefined the ultimate purpose of Israeli society. It was no longer a "blending of the Exiles," in other words, an elimination of the unique identity of the Jews who came from the Islamic world and their assimilation into the secular Ashkenazic mainstream. Instead, there was a concept of "togetherness," a multiplicity of cultural identities. As the economic situation of Moroccan Jews improved, there was a return to celebrating Mimouna largely with the family in the home. But other Sephardic communities took Mimouna as an example and created their own public ethnic celebrations, such as those of the Kurdish and Iranian Jews. Most recently, the Ethiopian community has added a holiday of its own. As the years have gone by, more and more Sephardic Jews have taken to making pilgrimages to the courts of famous rabbis, such as Baba Baruch in Netivot, and to the graves of Jewish saints throughout Israel, Egypt, and North Africa.

Many have gone to visit their childhood homes, especially in Morocco. David Ohana, a historian, wrote:

> I met happy Jews in Casablanca. . . . Next to Arab League Park on tree-lined Mulai Yosef Avenue, stands the building of the Education Association for Young Jews. . . . A soccer playoff game was in progress there, the climax of the Passover tournament between the club's teams. Some 5,000 fans and family members surrounded the field. It looked like a Club Med facility. Next to the fancy sports cars you can see Jews from overseas making passes at local Jewish girls. In the inner courtyard there was a relaxed atmosphere of communality.
>
> The club's president, Ama Levi, said proudly: 'This is the best community I know of. It's generous, has a great king and blessed soil.' He's an accountant, father of three, and spent three years living in Be'ersheva in Israel. 'I didn't like the mentality there, it's always pressured and people aren't polite. . . .

Thirty years after the revival of the Mimouna, Labor Party leader Shimon Peres analyzed the results of the 1996 election, which he lost to Benjamin Netanyahu. "What happened in these elections?" *Ha'aretz* correspondent Daniel Ben-Simon asked him. "We lost," Peres replied. "Who is 'we?'" Ben-Simon wanted to know. "'We' is the Israelis," Peres explained. "And who won?" Ben-Simon went on. "Those who don't have an Israeli mentality," Peres said. "Call them the Jews." He meant, of course, the Sephardic Jews. In those elections Shas, the ultra-Orthodox Sephardic party, increased its Knesset representation from six to ten seats. In the following elections, in 1999, it won seventeen seats.

Arieh Dayan, a journalist who writes about Shas, has spoken of "a new ultra-Orthodox Zionism." Yoel Nir, biographer of Shas political leader Aryeh Deri, called Shas, "the post-modernist response" to Labor, Likud, and the National Religious Party, which represents religious Zionism. Shas's rise is indeed a milestone along Israel's road from Zionism to Judaism, but the milestone before it was even more dramatic—Menachem Begin's accession to power in 1977. Begin came to power with Sephardic votes. They voted for him for a host of reasons. One is that they identified something Jewish in him, something undefined, not exactly conscious, but nevertheless more Jewish than Yitzhak Rabin and Yigal Alon, the avatars of the new Israeli, and even more Jewish than Shimon Peres.

Shas was born out of community work. Its activists first organized religion classes for children in disadvantaged neighborhoods in Jerusalem, where the schools suffered from discrimination and neglect. They also offered financial assistance for family needs, helping fund weddings, circumcisions, and other services that held together a poor population blighted by high levels of illiteracy and crime. This community effort was itself very Jewish; ultra-Orthodox Ashkenazis had created such community institutions long before, in the spirit of the social solidarity that had characterized Jewish enclaves in the Diaspora.

Shas's first battle was against Ashkenazic ultra-Orthodox discrimination. Most of the yeshivas with ties to Agudat Yisrael refused to accept Sephardic students, and the party did not want Sephardis in leadership positions. Some of the leaders of Shas cut their teeth on conflicts within the Ashkenazic ultra-Orthodox community. Some of them had studied in the few Ashkenazi yeshivas that had accepted them. Rabbi Ovadia Yosef assumed leadership of the new party after failing in his effort to win a second term as Israel's Sephardic chief rabbi.

Gradually, and at a relatively late stage, the movement took on anti-Zionist tendencies. "Zionism is a heretical movement that seeks to create a new Judaism," Aryeh Deri claimed, after the police began investigating him on charges of bribery. Those ultra-Orthodox Jews who think in historical-theological terms dream of a state governed by Halacha, Jewish religious law. For them, Zionist Israel can be no more than a transitional phase of marginal importance. Almost certainly, however, the majority of Shas voters would have difficulty identifying themselves as anti-Zionists. Deri's formulation was: "The real Zionists are us."

Shas's rhetoric frequently blurs concepts, perhaps part of its practice of melding political, social, and religious goals. It was Shas's leaders who introduced the word *elites* into Israel's political discourse, a modern incarnation of the term *establishment* in the 1960s. Both were deliberately imprecise and demagogic. Shas's attack on the "elites" put Israeli secular Zionism on the defensive and made it feel that it had never had as dangerous an adversary. The Sephardic party seems to challenge major elements of the Israeli identity of non-religious Jews, such as the authority of the Supreme Court and the freedom of the media. Shas has even begun to take an interest in the Holocaust, as some of its leaders have revived the old ultra-Orthodox accusation that the Zionists "abandoned" the Jews in Europe.

Many people in Palestine, leaders among them, displayed alienation when confronted with the news of the Jewish genocide. The catastrophe, they felt, was not theirs—the Holocaust was a defeat for Judaism, not Zionism. The new man was not, ostensibly, party to the calamity. Ironically, the institutionalized reaction of the Jewish community in Palestine was no different from the response of helpless, persecuted Jews of all times and in all places. The "new Hebrews" submitted petitions to the authorities, carefully worded to avoid indication of open rebellion. They "cried a great cry" at public meetings. They sent emissaries to other Jewish communities and tried to raise money from philanthropists. They prayed, fasted as a sign of mourning, and placed limits on the rejoicing allowed in family celebrations, following the pattern of rabbinic decrees issued during the Ukrainian pogroms of the seventeenth century.

In Israel's early years the Holocaust was a taboo of a sort. Survivors did not tell even their children what had happened to them, and their children dared not ask. This was the period of the great silence. Israelis were afraid of the survivors. They did not know how to integrate them into normal daily life at home, at work, on the bus, in line for the movies, on the beach. Holocaust survivors came from another world and, to the day they died, they were locked in an embrace with that other place. The tendency was to try to change them. "They must be imbued with a love of the homeland and the virtues of labor and human morality," said one leader. The survivors had to be given "fundamental human concepts," according to another. The survivors had to be "reeducated."

Many tried to describe what had happened to them, but words did not suffice. They found that Israelis were not willing or perhaps not able to listen. Hanzi Brand, widow of Joel Brand, who was involved in an attempt to rescue the Jews of Hungary, later recalled her first days at Kibbutz Givat Haim. Everyone was nice but no one wanted to hear her story. Instead, they told her what they had been through. The Arabs had attacked the farm and a shell had fallen on the chicken coop, they said over and over again. Brand's impression was that they talked about their war in order to avoid hers. She supposed they were ashamed of the Holocaust. She was not wrong.

Many were ashamed of the Jews' weakness; some were ashamed of the Zionist movement's inability to save them. Some blamed themselves for not doing more. Some blamed Europe's Jews for not having come to Palestine before the war. Over and over people asked the survivors how they had survived. By implication they were asking not how but why, and the question contained an insinuation of guilt. Ben-Gurion said: "Among the survivors of the German concentration camps were people who would not have prevailed had they not been what they are—hard, bad, and egotistical. And everything that happened to them excised all that is good from their souls." Again and again Israelis demanded that the survivors explain why they had not rebelled against the Nazis. The question embodied the new Hebrews image of themselves: they, the heroes, would not have gone like lambs to the slaughter.

Here and there the survivors made their own accusations against the Israelis. You didn't do all you could have done to save us, or at least encourage us, they said. The ultra-Orthodox community viewed the "abandonment" of European Jewry as evidence of the Zionist movement's evil character. Given all this, most everyone preferred simply not to talk about the Holocaust. So, until Adolf Eichmann's trial, few people did, even in the schools. The first curricula to set aside time for teaching the Holocaust were instituted in 1953. Two class periods were devoted to the subject.

Adolf Eichmann's abduction from Argentina and his trial in Jerusalem in 1961 were intended to promote several political objectives, both internal and external. Ben-Gurion needed proof that he was not apathetic about the Holocaust, despite his policy of reconciliation with Germany. Furthermore, Ben-Gurion's party had been badly damaged by both the Kastner trial of 1954, in which a Mapai activist had been accused of collaboration with the Nazis, and the Wadi Salib riots of 1959, in which poor Sephardic Jews had staged violent protests against the authorities. Ben-Gurion badly needed a purifying, unifying national experience to bring the country behind him again. Ben-Gurion also believed that Israel needed the trial to strengthen its claim to represent the entire Jewish people, including the victims of the Holocaust. There had even been a proposal to grant posthumous Israeli citizenship to all Holocaust victims, no matter where they might have been.

The principal impact of the Eichmann trial was unexpected. It set in motion a process of collective therapy for the entire country. Instead of being ashamed of the survivors and feeling superior to them, Israelis learned to identify with the victims' tragedy and internalize it as part of their identity. This identification was also expressed in the schools. In 1963 the Ministry of Education recommended devoting six class hours to study of the Holocaust.

The ability to identify with the victims grew more profound from year to year. In 1967, on the eve of the Six Day War, everyone spoke about the danger of the Arabs "exterminating Israel." The newspapers did not write that the Arabs would conquer the country or kill its citizens. The term used was the same one that described the Nazi genocide: *extermination*, thus speaking of a second Holocaust. President Gamal Abdal Nasser of Egypt was portrayed as Adolf Hitler. Prior to the war rabbis sanctified the country's public parks as cemeteries, assuming there would be hundreds of thousands of dead to bury. Only people who carried the memory of the Holocaust would thus anticipate the one to come. The tendency to look down on the Jews of Europe as weak began to change and eventually disappeared completely. Uri Praver, the army's deputy chief education officer, described the effect of the 1973 Yom Kippur War on consciousness of the Holocaust:

> The war showed all of us that Israel is not the most secure place in the world. In fact, it looked like a good invention that hadn't worked. I remember that someone wrote about the effect of Mark Spitz's success at the Olympics, that there was something profound in a Jewish kid from America swimming faster than the Jewish kid from Israel.
>
> The monolithic system we took with us from school—antisemitism-Zionism-security—that whole system cracked. For a few moments it looked as if it would collapse. In school, I remember, we were under the spell of the ghetto uprisings. We, the Israelis, would have been the fighters—even though we hadn't been born at the time—and they, the Jews, were the lambs to the slaughter. Suddenly that structure cracked. We needed the support of Jews in the United States. Not financial support—that was normal. Political support. Without them, we thought, we couldn't hold out. At that time there was, of course, a sense of total isolation.
>
> This was a basis for identification with precisely those people who had, up until then, been portrayed to us as "a den of decay and dust." So we rose up against the uprisings. After all, they were a symbol. We identified it with the big lie that the Yom Kippur War revealed to us. We had identified with the heroes. The war made us realize what the Holocaust meant and what the limitations of heroism were,

and we took our revenge against the symbol, the myth of the uprisings.

Many Israelis felt a similar sense of helplessness during the Gulf War in 1991. The common assumption was that the missiles Iraq fired at Israel were equipped with German-made gas. Iraq's president, Saddam Hussein, was identified with Hitler.

In time, the concept of heroism that Israelis had demanded of the Holocaust's victims also changed. As the years went by, they learned to appreciate not only the ghetto fighters and the partisans but also the heroes of passive resistance—the mother trying to obtain bread for her children, the theater troupe persisting with its performances, and other activities that preserved the victims' humanity. A textbook published at the end of the 1990s went so far as to omit all reference to the ghetto uprisings.

Consciousness of the Holocaust grew gradually until it became a central element of Israeli-Jewish identity. Innumerable surveys have confirmed this. Over the years research institutions, memorials, and museums have been established; not a day goes by without the Holocaust being mentioned at least once in some context or another in Israel's newspapers.

As the 1970s approached, the Ministry of Education formulated a sixty-lesson curriculum on the struggle for Israel's establishment. Ten of those lessons were devoted to the Holocaust. At the beginning of 1980 the Knesset amended the State Education Law. With the possible exception of the Declaration of Independence, this law is the Israeli collective's most authoritative credo, according to which the state's education is based on the following: "the cultural values of the people of Israel and their scientific achievements; love of the homeland and loyalty to the state and the Jewish people; training in agricultural work and trades; pioneer training and the aspiration for a society built on freedom, equality, tolerance, mutual assistance, and love for one's fellowman."

The 1980 amendment added the phrase "awareness of the Holocaust and its heroism." At this time the Holocaust became a mandatory part of the graduation examination in history, where it counts as 20 percent of a student's grade. Most Israeli students receive thirty hours of instruction in the Holocaust in elementary and secondary schools.

Thousands of Israeli teenagers have gone on class trips to the concentration camp sites in Poland. Some of these trips are more ritual in character, some more oriented toward study. The former emphasize the emotional experience, the latter, analysis and thought. Both programs are meant to deepen the teenagers' Jewish identity, and thus their patriotism. Holocaust consciousness has taken root primarily among non-religious Israelis, and some have even described it as an alternative to religion or a "civil religion." Either way, the Holocaust's ever-increasing importance has testified to an inner need among many for a renewal of their link to Jewish history and tradition.

Previously, the Holocaust played a relatively small role in the identities of religious and ultra-Orthodox Jews. Religion provided them with a way to forge a Jewish identity without it. Furthermore, they had great difficulty coping with the question of God's presence during the catastrophe. In recent years, however, there are indications that the religious and ultra-Orthodox communities are also developing a consciousness of the Holocaust. The process is very similar to that of non-religious Israelis and includes the establishment of institutes for research and documentation, teaching, and even religious and ultra-Orthodox memorials.

A fiery debate broke out in the executive committee of Israel's public broadcast authority in September 1978. The question was whether the country's sole television channel should broadcast the American miniseries *Holocaust*. Opponents described it as vulgar kitsch, but the broadcast was approved by a majority vote.

Changing awareness of the Holocaust reinforced a similar process occurring among American Jews. They had, however, made it a central element of their identity before Israelis did so. It became ever more important as American Jews grew less observant religiously and more secure as American citizens with equal rights. The Holocaust thus became a place where Israeli and American Jews could meet. Literally so, as thousands of teenagers meet during the March of the Living that takes place every two years at Auschwitz. The importance of the Holocaust in American Jewish identity is particularly notable because most U.S. Jews do not speak Hebrew and thus have no direct contact with Israeli culture.

In the early 1990s, the Ministry of Education instructed

teachers to focus their teaching of the Holocaust on individual figures, such as Janusz Korczak and Anne Frank. Numbers, the ministry explains, especially numbers in the millions, are meaningless and do not elicit strong emotions. The emphasis on the tragedy of the individual, in lieu of the national experience, is also a part of the individualist consciousness that new Zionist Israel imported from the United States.

And then the Russians came.

By the year 2000, Israel had taken in close to 1 million immigrants from the Soviet Union and its successor states: one Russian for every four Israelis. The mass immigration at the state's birth was greater than the resident population of Jews, thus its effect on society was more significant than the effect of this recent immigration. Yet, while it is still hard to pinpoint the affect on Israeli life, politics, and culture, clearly the Russian immigrants have reinforced the post-Zionist trend. In their countries of origin most had only the foggiest of connections to Israel and the Jewish people as a whole. The majority are secular.

Initial studies have shown a gradual decline in the force of Zionism as a motivating factor in their decision to settle in Israel. During the initial wave of Soviet immigration in the 1970s the Zionist motivation was dominant; in the 1990s it was marginal. A survey of candidates for immigration at the beginning of the decade showed that most Soviet Jews would have chosen some other country had they been given a choice.

They left their place of birth because life had become intolerable, and not just for Jews. Many came in the footsteps of relatives, but the choice of Israel was first and foremost the product of reduced immigrant quotas in the United States. The great majority have not relinquished their identification with Russian society and culture and continue to see it as a positive and important element in their self-image. Most speak Russian among themselves and with their children. They watch Russian satellite television broadcasts and read Russian newspapers and magazines, some of them published in Israel.

At the beginning of the 1980s the number of non-Jews among these immigrants began to rise. At one point it was estimated that half the newcomers from the former Soviet Union were not Jewish. These people swell the non-Zionist population of Israel, which is also growing because of the ultra-Orthodox high birth rate, twice that of non-religious Jews. Then add the hundreds of thousands of foreign workers now residing in the country. Because they supposedly reside on a temporary basis only, and since they are generally easily visible, many Israelis ignore them as if they will vanish the same way they appeared. Yet many, perhaps even most, will in the end settle in Israel permanently, just as they have in Europe. They, too, are one of the factors that has hastened the post-Zionist era.

In the year 2000 some 35 percent of all Israeli children were not enrolled in Hebrew-Zionist schools. About a quarter of Israel's children are Arabs, and another 20 percent study outside the framework of the national school system, the great majority in ultra-Orthodox institutions. They dwell in a state entirely different than that of the Zionist dream. Inevitably, Israelis have also begun to think differently. This new thinking stands out in a pair of articles written by two of *Ha'aretz*'s editors.

In the summer of 1985, *Ha'aretz* Editor-in-Chief Gershom Schocken called on Israel to encourage mixed marriages between Jews and Arabs. Intermarriage, he claimed, would create a true Israeli nation. He called his article "The Curse of Ezra," referring to the Jewish leader who returned from Babylonia to Zion to rebuild the Temple. Ezra prohibited Jews from marrying Gentiles. Schocken wrote:

> When the founders of Zionism embarked on reestablishing Jews as a nation, an independent political force just like the rest of the family of nations, they did not notice that the prohibition against intermarriage could create problems for the Jewish nation returning to its land. . . . This awareness has still not penetrated the public consciousness. But the fact is that there is no sovereign people in the world that forbids marriage with the members of other peoples. On the contrary, nearly all European nations (not to speak of the Americans) were created by the blending of a variety of peoples. . . .
>
> To ensure the emergence of an Israeli nation that will include all the country's ethnic groups, we must tear down the walls between them, and that includes the restrictions on intermarriage. Had we not granted the rabbinate a monopoly

in the area of personal status and had we enacted a civil marriage law, a serious obstacle would have been removed. . . .
For a sovereign nation that must achieve coexistence with the
members of another group and create normal relations with
neighbors beyond its borders, this prohibition, which symbolizes alienation between the Jews and other groups, has
become a curse. If it continues, it will contribute to making
permanent the tension within the country and its isolation
in the region.

Some nine years later, another *Ha'aretz* editor, Hanoch Marmari, proposed to limit the Law of Return and that it cease to
apply on the seventy-fifth anniversary of Israel's independence,
that is, in May 2023. To quote at length:

The centrality of the Law of Return, its necessity and its
inviolability, derived the existential needs of a small community that rose up to declare itself a state. The ingathering
of the Diaspora was necessary to reach a critical mass of Jewish
population, to create a demographic advantage over the country's Arab inhabitants and allow the construction of an independent defense force and economy. . . .

Forty-six years after establishing the country, the trou-
bled Diaspora has emptied out and the better-off ones have
fallen silent. . . . Toward the end of the decade and the century, Israel will have five million Jews and no Jewish communities will remain in most of the countries where they
were a persecuted minority . . . The problematic nature of a

state law based on religious immigration has created distortions over the years; the distortions barely noticeable during mass immigration will return to irk us the moment every immigrant is examined individually. Who has the greater right to live here as a citizen—a 'Black Hebrew' [a Christian cult that arrived in Israel in the 1970s] who has lived in Israel for 25 years and has remained loyal out of a religious faith that is not Jewish (and who is to this day prevented from becoming an Israeli citizen), or an Ethiopian descended from Jews who converted to Christianity? What about the rights of a Romanian who builds the country as a temporary worker and has in the meantime married and wishes to tie his fate to Israel? Or does a baby who was circumcised this morning in Des Moines, Iowa have a greater right? What about the right of a Korean computer genius who works at the Weizmann Institute against the right of a pensioner who is the son of an alleged Jew from Novosibirsk? . . .

Limiting the duration of the Law of Return means declaring that the law—unlike the state—is a temporary mechanism. Admitting the temporary nature of the Law of Return constitutes a recognition of the state's 'eternal nature.' The day it goes out of force will be the official end of the Zionist movement's mission; the movement will be able to dismantle itself having fulfilled its mission with impressive if not complete success. . . . in addition to a Jewish people and a Jewish religion and a Jewish minority in any number of countries, there will also be a country of Jews, sovereign and normal, speaking Hebrew, in which other minorities live. This will be the end of the weighty paradox of a country that defines its population according to Orthodox religious law. . . . This will not be the end of the strong and special ties the Jewish state feels toward the Jews of the world; all cultural and institutional links can continue and even become stronger. . . . The State of Israel is now home to a varied ethnic, cultural, and religious population, which is in the process of defining itself and its needs, and the immigration policy of a developed country should derive from the needs of its citizens.

The two articles in *Ha'aretz* show that the most innovative ideas have come from the press not from the academic world. Indeed, the principal theater of operations in the Israeli culture wars, including the battles over history, has not been the universities. It has been the Knesset and the media.

FACING
GADI MANELLA'S
STATUE

"There Is No Honor"

At the entrance to Kibbutz Tel Yitzhak, not far from the local Holocaust museum, there is a bronze statue of Gadi Manella. Born and raised on the kibbutz, Manella was killed as a soldier in June 1968 while chasing down terrorists in the Jordan Valley. The statue is by Natan Rapaport, a sculptor who occupies a special place in Israel's culture of memory. More than anyone, he is responsible for its Stalinist flavor. The statues he placed at Kibbutz Negba and Kibbutz Yad Mordecai and elsewhere were works in the official style of the Soviet Union, in the 1940s and 1950s still a "second homeland" for many Israelis. By the time he fashioned Manella's memorial, Rapaport no longer resided in Joseph Stalin's Soviet Union. He lived in Toronto.

A member of the kibbutz had acquaintances in Canada who

agreed to pay the sculptor's fee of $15,000. Manella's statue was also meant to memorialize Colonel Arik Regev, who was killed in the same skirmish. It stands on a boulder brought from the spot where the two men fell. About six feet high, the whole work is more or less life-size. Manella, in a paratrooper's uniform, projects peace and an unexpected gentleness, very different from Rapaport's previous memorials. The limbs are thin, slightly overlong; the head is a bit too small; the face almost that of a child. His two arms are raised before him, one with a gap between the ring and middle fingers, as in the Jewish priestly blessing, and the other as if commanding the Arabs to halt. The kibbutz members stipulated that the paratrooper's rifle be hidden. The statue depicts an eternal Jewish boy, a kind of Israeli Peter Pan a moment before he takes off for heaven. The Tel Yitzhak sculptor was attempting to convey a message of national unity. But unity has slipped out of reach. The fissures in society in fact deepened precisely when peace seemed to be at hand.

One evening in 1993, some sixty thousand demonstrators massed outside the prime minister's office in Jerusalem. They had come to protest the Oslo accords signed with the Palestine Liberation Organization. That same evening sixty thousand other Israelis assembled in Tel Aviv—for a Michael Jackson concert. Jerusalem is a religious city, political, intolerant, even fanatic, five thousand years old, and built on rock. Tel Aviv is built on sand. It hasn't yet had its hundredth birthday, and its residents live free and easy—not for the past, not for the future, but for life itself. They are part of the "now" culture they've imported from America. There's something ironic in the fact that Jerusalem, once the stronghold of opposition to Zionism, has become a symbol of Israeli patriotism, while Tel Aviv, once Zionism's capital, its patriotic redoubt, has become the bastion of post-Zionist identity. Religion is identified with Judaism, and Judaism with the political right; secularism is identified with the left. In this sense, Yitzhak Rabin's assassin chose the wrong city for his crime. Spiritually and politically, Rabin was murdered in, and in the name of, Jerusalem.

"Two shots," novelist Eli Amir wrote, "instantly turned Yitzhak Rabin into a myth. The mourning for this Sabra, this native-born Israeli, revealed something surprising about Israel's children—they are a generation that seeks peace and are as turbulent and reserved as the towering grandfather figure they were crying for. The murder shattered their dream and ripped their father figure from them. . . . This generation stood behind him and behind the hope he represented."

Amir was referring to the "candle kids." Within hours after Rabin's murder they filled the sidewalks—thousands of teenage boys and girls, sitting in circles around flickering candles. Guitars and naive graffiti were their instruments of mourning, symbols and rituals from 1960s America mixed with the ambience they'd absorbed from their older siblings' stories of post-army backpacking trips to India. In the memories of older Israelis, Rabin's assassination took its place alongside John F. Kennedy's. "Yitzhak Rabin was a red-haired boy with beautiful eyes who seemed born to be the poster child of the Hebrew revolution," wrote novelist and critic Amos Kenan. But the revolution was caught up in a crisis brought on in part by the first Palestinian uprising, the *intifada* of the late 1980s.

In its second year, sociologists and students of public opinion were already pointing to indications that the *intifada* was causing the fissures in Israeli society to grow wider. They also noted that, for the first time, cracks were appearing in the solid front that had opposed negotiations with the PLO. There were the first signs of a weariness that later became more profound. Sixty percent of Israelis said that the situation in the occupied territories caused them "a certain measure" of fatigue; 16 percent said they were "entirely worn out;" 24 percent said they weren't fatigued at all. The most notable weariness was registered among respondents who identified themselves as people of the left. After them came Arabs, then right-wingers, army officers, and religious people. Among those who said they were entirely worn out, some wanted to leave the country while others spoke of refusing to perform military service in the territories, something that presented many Israelis, among them soldiers and officers, with a moral dilemma.

The media, which had adopted the American media's value system, amplified the feeling that the disturbances required new thinking. That was the Palestinians' great achievement. They did not defeat the army, but they made Israelis sick of ruling the West Bank and Gaza Strip. Something similar had happened during the British Mandate: the British put down the great Arab revolt that broke out in the mid-1930s, but the Arabs succeeded in making them sick of Palestine.

• • •

Two years after Rabin's assassination, several old-timers from Hamahanot Haolim assembled at Kibbutz Beit Hashita. Hamahanot Haolim, a youth movement, had established a number of kibbutzim. After the Six Day War, many of its members were among the founders of the Greater Israel movement. They were the secular messianists of Israeli rule over the West Bank and Gaza Strip.

The participants in the reunion gathered to talk about the death of their dream. One of them placed the reunion in its historical context: "Thirty years after the Six Day War, twenty-five years after the Yom Kippur War. Long years of wars, long periods of disputes, short periods of consensus over the fundamental idea—realizing our rights to Greater Israel."

The discussion was very personal. The Land of Israel stood at the center of these people's lives; it was an object of love, a means of self-realization. Waking up from that dream was, as they describe it, a process of maturation and of aging. Ideological fervor had waned; awareness of realities grew. The same may have happened to Yitzhak Rabin. Aliza Badmor of Kibbutz Kabri said:

> The countryside we saw on our hikes didn't address the Arabs or the country's political future. They urged a concept in which the word 'wholeness' was the key. Seeing the whole panorama. The mountains crowning the valleys. The land

stretching from the Mediterranean to the Sea of Galilee. The desert with its wadis and water holes and the jutting prominence of Masada. . . . We internalized the land as a total experience. In the youth movement there was an unambiguous truth: 'this is the way, there is no other, come and walk it, walk it to the very end.' But that gave way to coping with life itself, and coping with life itself is, among other things, discerning shades, complexities, and perhaps more than that.

Azaria Alon said:

I grew up on the concept of a Land of Israel that had no boundaries. It's map that included both banks of the Jordan, Mount Hermon, the Druze Mountain in Syria, and the lands of Gilad, Moab, and Edom in Jordan. The Mandatory borders were certainly evident, but there was this concept of the Land of Israel. . . . There was a huge contradiction between what we actually had and what we felt attached to. . . . While we could not visit all parts of the land, there was no place we thought we had no right to go, whether it was the Judean Desert, the northern border, the Jordan River, the mountains of Samaria, the craters in the Negev. We tried to reach every place and we had some sense of ownership, a sense of belonging to the entire land. . . .

No one thought of conquest by force or expulsion of the Arabs, but there was this vague hope that a day would come when we would be the majority, and then . . . That's where the hope ended: 'and then.' So things continued until the summer of 1967. I don't know of any serious person who planned to change Israel's borders by force. What did we all dream of? That was left to the dreams of each individual.

. . . I never lost the Land of Israel . . . even though I did not know how, whether, and when my feet would again tread in those places. In my mind I still belonged to them, perhaps like the Jew who always had the Land of Israel somewhere in the back of his mind. The State of Israel was a reality, the Land of Israel was in the realm of the imagination. . . . Yet I and those who thought like me could not give up the Land of Israel, even as we lived in a country named Israel.

On Independence Day, most of the years between 1959 and 1967, I would devote a talk on the radio to a site or scenic point on the other side of the border . . . That got people mad. In 1967, two weeks before the war broke out, I talked about Wadi Kelt, near Jericho. Someone came up to me, very mad, and asked me why I was talking about such places. A week later he came to me and said: "You knew!" . . . We went on hikes all over the West Bank, and I was drunk, I returned to places I had known and went to places I hadn't known. . . .

. . . I never thought of the places in the West Bank where the Arabs live as foreign to me—not Nablus, not Jenin, not Jericho. It doesn't pain me that the Arabs live there, because they are part of the land. . . . Today it's clear to me that there's a Palestinian people and that it lives here and that we cannot have a binational state and that we can't maintain a state with 4.5 million Jews and 4 million Arabs. Little by little the recognition that we need to divide it seeped in. How to divide it? If only I knew. We're talking about settlements. I think some of the settlements they established in Judea and Samaria have to go, and clear lines have to be drawn.

I'm not parting with the Land of Israel. Whether I can hike through it or I can't hike through it. . . . I don't know what "Greater Israel" is because I know that never in the history of this land did we live in all of it nor were we the masters of it all, and if there were periods like that they were very brief, even David's kingdom. . . . Whoever wants to run away can run away, but we will have to divide this country. But when we do that I don't lose the land—it remains mine.

This, then, is the ideological foundation for the policy of separation, which in essence means partition. The poet Haim Guri, one of the signatories of the Greater Israel movement's declaration in 1967 and later a wholehearted supporter of Rabin's Oslo initiative, also participated in the gathering at Beit Hashita. He recounted his journey from a dream of conquest to the reality of occupation.

I too was part of those treks, of that love. The youth movement and army hikes added something precious to the ancient link between the Jewish people and the Land of Israel. They were part of our collective biography. They took place under the fierce sun, in salt and thirst, in wind and rain, an ongoing rite of passage of people entering into a covenant with the land, discovering it, its landscape and its seasons. Geography and history. We were bursting with the irrepressible youthful joy that comes out of toil and work and reaching for the highest goals. . . .

I have never seen and do not see the Jewish people as an occupier in its own land. But we have for decades ruled over another people. No, it is not occupation, but it is rule by force over an extended period that oppresses another nation, with all that implies. Today I know what I did not suppose then, at the beginning of the encounter of the peoples between the Jordan and the sea. Many among us sought to do what was best for the nation under our rule and did so. But many did what was bad in the eyes of God and man. And so there was the cheap Arab labor and appalling exploitation. A society that in the past sanctified Hebrew labor became a society of bosses and hardened slavedrivers in need of working hands.

When the Arabs overcame their initial period of shock, resistance to our rule began. It became more and more violent and necessarily led to ever more severe responses, to searches and raids and arrests, to curfews and closures, to harsh interrogations, to beatings, to tear gas, to rubber bullets, to live bullets, to punitive operations, to blowing up houses and, yes, alas, to abuse and humiliations that served no military purpose.

These things came in response to the hostility and the curses and the terror and the mass demonstrations that shouted "Oh Jews, Mohammed's army will return!" They were drawn on by the stabbings, the ambushes, and the deadly bombs in our homes and streets. An army that overcame the strongest and best-armed Arab armies had trouble finding its way through the appallingly poor neighborhoods of the refugee camps. Soldiers found themselves involved in brutal incidents. They did not shoot to kill, but more than once, in the heat of the fight, women and children were hurt by accident. And so, while they still needed to make their livings here among us just as they needed to breathe, on the scaffolds and in the orchards and in the greenhouses, in the restaurants and the cafés, they broadcast an image of being an ever-present threat, of suspicion and hatred. They also took part in cruel acts of violence that again and again led to closures and curfews, to the point that many barely had food to eat.

Haim Guri continued:

Many believed that Yitzhak Rabin was blazing a trail to a different future in the Land of Israel and in the region. They accepted a painful compromise. . . . We are trying to answer the vexing question: "When did we part with Greater Israel?" . . . We never ceased to love it to the very last of its stones, we never ceased to believe unreservedly in the Jewish people's right to the Land of Israel, its only treasure. But this reality created between the Jordan and the sea after the Six Day War taught us the hard way that only a compromise of separation and partnership will make life possible here and perhaps bring succor to this stricken region. The rule over another nation corrupts and distorts Israel's qualities, tears the nation apart, and shatters society.

Rabin internalized this new spirit. He shook the hand of the man who had only recently, for many Israelis and perhaps for Rabin himself, been an incarnation of Adolf Hitler. He handed to him Palestinian cities that many Israelis, and perhaps Rabin himself, had once considered vital for the country's defense.

But the candle kids, Israel's Peter Pans, construed Rabin's murder as an attack on an apolitical Israel that had stopped living as a mobilized, fighting collective. For them, the murder threatened the private dream of each and every individual. Rabin was not their hero before the assassination; their values were not his. Yet "they eulogized him in tears and in song, a song for peace," Eli Amir wrote.

Amir was referring to a specific song of that name. The story of the "Song for Peace" is the story of Israeli identity. The lyrics were written by Ya'akov Rotblit, who lost one of his legs as a soldier in the Six Day War. His song was one of the first manifestations of Israeli Americanization. Words like "Let the sun shine through the flowers" and "Sing a song to love and not to war" were born in the Vietnam antiwar movement. For many years it was a protest song that expressed the sentiments only of the fringe. At the time the song came out, General Rehavam Ze'evi of Israel's Central Command forbid the army entertainment troupe in his region to sing it.

The fact that the words were sung by Yitzhak Rabin just minutes before he was murdered shows just how far Israeli society had traveled since the Six Day War, when Rabin had been the army's chief of staff. It is extremely doubtful that he had identified with the song then.

At the beginning of the 1980s, the government began declassifying documents from the state's early years. For the first time it became possible to study the country's history. Israel is relatively liberal in this regard—there are countries that don't open their archives at all. But until the first files were opened the state's history could not be researched. Most of the books that claimed to tell Israel's story were official and semiofficial summaries such as *The Haganah History Book*, many of them published by the Ministry of Defense, as were the books issued by various organizations, including the underground militias of preindependence days and political parties. Over the years a number of memoirs were published by people who had been involved in events. One of these figures, David Ben-Gurion, was not satisfied with having made history; he aspired to be the historian of his era as well.

Statesmen and governments frequently voice historical justifications for their policies, but Israel needed history to justify its very establishment. "The Bible is our title deed," Ben-Gurion declared when he appeared before one of the commissions of inquiry the British sent to Palestine from time to time. That, in essence, is the Zionist claim in a nutshell. The Jewish people were exiled from their land and are now returning to it to renew their days as of old. Israeli history is thus of existential importance. Accordingly, the Zionist Organization funded a book written by Ben-Zion Dinaburg (Dinur) *Israel in Its Land*. The goal was "to uproot the mistaken concept that the Jews' exile from their land was complete and that the Arabs found a land free of Jews." Dinaburg stated that the country lost its "Jewish character" only in the seventh or eighth century, that is, when the Arabs arrived. He thus shortened the Exile by about one thousand years and linked it to the Arab conquest. Dinaburg put an emphasis on Jewish historical continuity and the unity of the entire nation, as if there were but one narrative and a single series of events in the history of a people.

From time to time the Zionist movement funded studies meant to prove that most Arabs had come to Palestine only recently. Ben-Gurion once tried to prove that the Arab peasants were actually descendants of the ancient Israelites. He intended to buttress the idea others had also proposed, according to which Jews had continued to practice agriculture even after they had lost their independence.

Zionist historiography was meant not only to prove the justice of the cause to the non-Jewish world but also to reinforce Zionism's somewhat tenuous position among the Jews themselves. The official in charge of the schooling of immigrant Yemenite children said the goal of their education was to impress on them "the magic of the state" and make each one "a reliable partner in the colossal, great, and wonderful Israeli revolution, whose expression is the State of Israel and its accomplishments."

Archival material declassified at the beginning of the 1980s included the internal correspondence of government ministries, among them the Foreign Ministry and the prime minister's office, as well as the files of the Jewish Agency. Ben-Gurion's diary was also opened for inspection. Israel's founding fathers wrote a lot. It turned out there was quite a bit of difference between what they said and wrote for public consumption and what they did, wrote, said, and apparently also thought among themselves. These records are the essence of the new history. The documents created the new history, not an ideological urge to slander the Zionist movement. What occured was an encounter, usually numbing—first and foremost for the historian—with documents that had previously been inaccessible.

In early 1949, for example, the Jews of Poland were allowed to emigrate to Israel. The government had to address the question of where they would be housed when they arrived. The Jewish Agency's executive board discussed the matter. During that same period tens of thousands of immigrants from Arab countries were living in transit camps, but a decision was made to house the newcomers from Poland in hotels. "The immigrants include people of standing and it would be a scandal if we have to send them to the camps," said one member of the Jewish Agency. A colleague explained: "If we exempt the Polish Jews from the camps and give them preference, they will manage better than most of the oriental Jews in the camps, because many of them have professions much in demand. . . . This will bring benefit to the national economy." One participant in the discussion reminded his colleagues that the immigrants had to be helped simply because they were from Poland, just like some members of the Executive. "We're from the same tribe," he said. Later on the members discussed how they could conceal their decision from the press. When the minutes were made public decades later, many Israelis were deeply shocked. After all, the official truth was that there had been no discrimination against Jews from the Arab world. The revelations gave impetus to oriental Jewish social and political protest movements.

Official truth also had it that Israel did everything to pursue negotiations with its Arab neighbors, and they had refused to talk to Israel. Many were astonished when it turned out, also at the beginning of the 1980s, that Syrian president Husni Za'im had asked, almost pleaded, to meet with Ben-Gurion in 1949. Za'im intended to offer a peace agreement under which Syria would absorb between 300 million and 350 million Palestinian refugees as permanent residents. In return, Ben-Gurion wrote in his diary, the Syrians demanded "half of the Sea of Galilee." He refused to meet with Za'im, who was murdered a short time later, so it can't be said that Israel missed a historic opportunity for peace and a resolution to the Palestinian refugee problem. It can be said, however, that the Ben-Gurion government hid the truth from the public.

Innumerable documents made available to the public over the years, touching on a large number of issues, showed that Israel's history was less beautiful, less noble, less innocent, less just, and less wise than the country had always claimed. They also revealed many "gray areas," because, in contrast to the impression created before the archives were opened, Israeli history did not take place in a world where everything was black and white. Quite naturally, when the truth was uncovered, there was a debate about the policies the official myths were meant to justify.

Many of the papers uncovered in the archives cast new light on the War of Independence and the birth of the refugee problem. Israel had always denied that it wanted to get rid of the Arabs and that it had engaged in expulsions. On the contrary, according to the official record during the War of Independence the Haganah's commanders had done their best to persuade the Arabs to remain. But what researchers found were not only explicit expulsion orders but also evidence of war crimes committed by Israeli soldiers, including murder, torture, rape, and looting. In the minutes of one meeting that remained classified but were leaked to a historian, a minister compared these war crimes to those of the Nazis.

Another revelation was that several Zionist leaders had consistently advocated population transfer—moving Palestine's

Arab population, or at least part of it, outside Israel's borders, or at least outside certain parts of the country. The transfer was variously envisioned as taking place voluntarily, by agreement, by force, or some combination. Until then it had been convenient to believe that the concept of transfer was an American import brought over by Rabbi Meir Kahane, or that it belonged exclusively to the far-right Moledet party led by Rehavam Ze'evi. When the archives were opened, it turned out that the concept had, in fact, been tossed around at the very center of the Zionist movement. It had been accepted by Theodor Herzl, and, much more important, advocated by David Ben-Gurion. The historical documentation that exists today points to a clear link between the concept of population transfer and the creation of the Arab refugee problem. Most of the inhabitants who left their homes did so as war loomed, or fled in fear from battle. About half of them were expelled, although generally at the initiative of local commanders, not as part of a general program of deportation.

There were those who warned Ben-Gurion that the refugee problem would plague Israel for years to come. "We still do not properly comprehend what an enemy we are now raising outside our country's borders," one government minister said. "Our enemies in the Arab countries are utterly insignificant in comparison with the thousands of Palestinians who will, out of deliberate hostility and lack of an alternative and abysmal hatred storm our country despite any settlement we might reach." Ben-Gurion thought that the problem would solve itself: some refugees would be absorbed by the Arab countries, some would become accustomed to their fate, others would die. Ben-Gurion devoted his entire life to his people's national aspirations but never managed to understand that the yearning to return home would mold the national identity and enmity of the Palestinian refugees. This may well have been his greatest failure as a statesman. Either way, in time it became impossible to ignore the Palestinians, partly because they began, as some had predicted back in 1949, organizing terrorist attacks against Israel, hijacking airplanes, and exploding car bombs in city centers.

By the early 1980s, Israel had developed a fairly established tradition of protest against the country's defense policies. At the end of the 1950s and at the beginning of the 1960s there had been a campaign to abolish the military government under which Israel's Arab citizens lived in the northern and southern parts of the country. A massacre at Kfar Kassem in 1956, when Israeli soldiers murdered unarmed villagers, gave impetus to that struggle, as did the country's first major political scandal, the Lavon affair.

Then Israeli rule over the territories conquered in the Six Day War produced ever-increasing protest against violations of Palestinian human rights. A group of twelfth-graders sent a letter to Prime Minister Golda Meir in April 1970 saying they could not serve in the army wholeheartedly because the government was not exhausting every opportunity to reach a peace agreement with the Arabs. This was a milestone; the public was beginning to criticize defense policy. The Yom Kippur War irreparably destroyed the widespread belief that the government could be trusted to defend the country properly. Later, mass right-wing demonstrations tried to prevent Israel's withdrawal from the Sinai Peninsula, carried out in fulfillment of the country's commitments in its peace treaty with Egypt. In 1982, the Lebanon War provoked mass demonstrations from the other side of the political spectrum. The Oslo agreement was met with protests that climaxed with Rabin's assassination.

By the time the new historians published their first books, Israeli society had thus experienced a whole series of political and ideological "earthquakes"; skepticism and protest at times seemed to bring the country to the brink of civil war. Yoram Hazony, an Israeli scholar who grew up in the United States and who worked for a time for Benjamin Netanyahu, argued that the new historians were just the latest outbreak of a disease infecting the Israeli intellectual community since the country's inception. In 2000 Hazony published a sweeping critique of Israeli intellectual history titled *The Jewish State: The Struggle for Israel's Soul*.

Post-Zionism was born together with Zionism, Hazony charges. Just as Zionism's founding father was Theodor Herzl, post-Zionism's ancestor was Ahad Ha'am, the Hebrew essayist who opposed Herzl's political dreams, preferring instead a cultural center—but not a sovereign state—in Palestine. According to Hazony, Ahad Ha'am's ideas were taken up by the scholars who formed the founding nucleus of the Hebrew

University of Jerusalem, people like Judah Leib Magnes and Martin Buber. These intellectuals, most of them of German origin, founded Ihud and Brit Shalom, two organizations that advocated binational—that is, non-Zionist—solutions to the conflict over Palestine.

These scholars were the teachers of the first generation of native intellectuals and, through them, of Israel's current educated elite. The result, Hazony claims, has been that most educated Israelis today, even the majority who consider themselves Zionists and patriots, are in fact infected by post-Zionism.

"The real subject," Hazony writes, "is the mainstream of Jewish cultural figures in Israel—those who appear constantly on television as commentators on subjects of national importance, whose books are best-sellers and are taught in the public schools, who attend parties in the homes of Israel's leading politicians, and who serve on government committees. . . . I recognize that these are in many cases people who call themselves Zionists and are proud to be Israelis. . . . [But in] my view, it is these establishment cultural figures, even more than the circles of the self-professed post-Zionists, who are today paving the way to the ruin of everything Herzl and the other leading Zionists sought to achieve."

One dangerous manifestation of this infection, Hazony has argued, is that consciously and unconsciously post-Zionist historians have been weakening the national consciousness of Israeli youth through the textbooks and curricula they have devised for secondary schools. In his book, in a series of articles, and in a glossy pamphlet produced by the Shalem Center, the think tank he heads, Hazony has made a detailed critique of the way history is taught in schools.

Predictably, the sharpest reaction to Hazony's claims has come not from the post-Zionist new historians but from mainstream scholars who have themselves been critics of the new history. They were profoundly insulted and incensed when Hazony lumped them together with the very people they criticize. Prominent among them is Israel Bartal of the Hebrew University, who oversaw production of the textbook that attracted the bulk of Hazony's ire. Bartal published a response in which he, in turn, accused Hazony of carrying out "an anti-Zionist propaganda campaign" and presenting "a hostile, false, and absolutely distorted view of Israeli culture, the Israeli educational system, and Israel's institutions of higher education."

As with Hazony, Bartal's ideological roots lie in the classic labor Zionism of David Ben-Gurion. Hazony claims that Bartal has betrayed that tradition; Bartal accuses Hazony of exactly the same thing, claiming that his goal is to demonstrate that, "everything we thought was Zionist up until now is anti-Zionist. In other words, we are all 'new historians,' we are all 'post-Zionists,' we all sin by not fitting Dr. Hazony's definition of Zionism." Hazony's claim is so dreadful, in Bartal's opinion, that the Ministry of Education ought to sue him for libel. The good Zionist Bartal was insulted because Hazony attacked him from the right, as if *he* were the greater patriot. But Hazony is in fact correct; approaches once considered provocative found their way into a number of textbooks. Bartal is right as well, however; most textbooks still reflect a fairly conservative Israeli Zionism.

It is significant that both Hazony and Bartal look back to the age of Ben-Gurion and labor Zionist dominance as the forge of national values. The labor movement's credo of pioneering self-sacrifice and collective identity were essential to the creation of the Jewish state and were the dominant ethos of its formative years, even if never adopted in practice by most Israelis. People who took those values seriously—the young who in the 1940s and 1950s established new settlements in far-off places, who fought in the ranks of the prestate underground and the army—are the grandparents of early-twenty-first-century Israel. Once they were the elite; now they find that the values to which they sacrificed their youth are under attack. No one represents them better than another labor Zionist, novelist Aharon Megged, who says that the new historiography is the product of a "death wish."

In 1994 Megged published an article in *Ha'aretz*'s weekend magazine stating that books by the new Historians were written in the spirit of Zionism's "enemies and opponents." In his essay, "The Israeli Urge to Suicide," Megged wrote that "the only conclusion to be drawn from these studies and articles is that the . . . Zionist program was an evil 'colonialist' plot to exploit the Palestinian nation, enslave it, deprive it of its land, replace it."

Megged gave details:

The message is that most of our certainties are lies. You, whose parents came from Poland and settled in a small village and worked hard and built a tiny farm—you thought they came here to . . . create a new life in the land of their forefathers, a life of labor and Hebrew culture, free from the fear of pogroms and dependence on the gentiles. Sorry, you were wrong! You were naive! They were 'colonialists' whose secret desire was to exploit the Arabs in the village next door!

You, who in your youth, after you finished your studies, labored in the citrus groves, in construction, in fishing, at the port, you thought you were engaging in the 'conquest of labor' . . . making the Jewish people into a nation that lived off the labor of its hands—you deceived yourself! You did it to push aside the native Arab laborers! When you joined a kibbutz and settled desolate sands and began to grow vegetables and fruit trees—you probably thought you were 'redeeming the land' and 'making the desert bloom' and all that. But no! You stole the peasants' land, which had been bought by the Jewish National Fund!

And when you were in the army and did guard duty, when every day and every night Jews were murdered by ambushes and orchards were uprooted and fields set on fire,

and you restrained yourself and did not take revenge on innocent Arabs, you thought you were observing the moral imper-
ative you were taught in school and in your youth movement
and in the labor movement. But no! . . .

Megged cites historian Ilan Pappe's review of historian
Anita Shapira's book *Land and Power: The Zionist Resort to Force,
1881–1948,*:

Zionism can be analyzed as a colonialist movement and its
uniqueness is only in its historical timing. It is not unique
in what it did to the local population, in the way it uprooted
it, exploited it, as it continues to do in the occupied territories.

Whoever someday studies the dimensions of this patho-
logical phenomenon—whose origins lie, perhaps, in the
Diaspora Jewish habit of self-abnegation and groveling before
those who hate us—will have to wade through a huge
amount of material. Thousands of articles, hundreds of
poems, songs, and satires, dozens of documentary and narrative films, exhibitions and paintings and photographs that
depict Israeli soldiers as Nazi troopers. . . . All these, when
taken together, make up a monstrous indictment of Israel,
much more venomous and sophisticated than any of the more
or less primitive Palestinian propaganda distributed throughout the world. . . . And thus Israeli Jews carry out Jesus's
command from the Sermon on the Mount: "Love your enemies, bless them that curse you . . . and persecute you," that

very same precept the Christian world has not succeeded in observing for two thousand years. . . .

If this rising tide that challenges our right to be here in our historic homeland does not ebb . . . we will not have the strength to face the dangers that threaten our very existence.

To a large measure, those who think like Megged and those who take a more critical approach are engaged in a battle between two generations.

The Zionist movement tried to defend itself. The World Zionist Organization published a work, *Judaism as a Culture*, by Eliezer Schweid, a professor at the Hebrew University, who linked post-Zionism with postmodernism. Like postmodernists, post-Zionists cannot attach themselves to any alternative ideology, so they look to history, Schweid wrote. Their work, he argued, does not offer conclusions that address the future of the Jewish people or of the State of Israel. That's understandable, he wrote: "Post-Zionist ideology has no foundation in a culture of its own that its representatives identify with. From where they stand as individuals, objective history is shunted aside . . . into a 'dead area' and disappears. As scholars, they have only the subjective interests of individuals who are alienated from their own nation. . . . It turns out, then, that they flee from collective self-identity and deny biographical-historical identity and pull the foundations out from under all responsible thinking about the future."

Schweid was right. There is no unified formulation of post-Zionist ideology. But the debate over Zionism's past is anchored, of course, in the debate over Israel's future. Ilan Pappe wrote a response to Megged's article:

> We will continue to debate the image of Israel as an established fact that was created as a means of saving Jews, but at the heavy price of the destruction of the Palestinian culture and homeland. I will continue to argue that we must resolve the serious contradiction between a Zionist and Jewish statehood and civil rights and democracy, not just as a way of repairing the injustices of the past, but mostly to make normal life in the future possible. A democratic and pluralist Israel as part of the Mediterranean basin is also an Israel of varied historical narratives, of more than one truth. Such an Israel bears hope for a common future. The debate will continue to be sustained by moral positions, the methodology of historical writing from ideological positions.

The debate extends beyond Israel's borders. The media in nearly every other country has covered it, and some American and European universities have made it a subject of conferences and books. The large amount of attention that the new historians have garnered is more than they deserve and may well reflect the huge difficulty of conceptualizing the Israeli culture war. The new historians' books have provided a convenient framework for doing so. For the most part, the books and their authors were engaging in a political debate, even when it seemed they had no connection with current events. Such was the case with Israel Yuval and Ze'ev Herzog.

Israel Yuval of the Hebrew University published an article at the end of 1993 in the journal *Zion* on the *Av Harahamim* prayer. This prayer, recited in synagogues on the Sabbath, calls on God to take revenge against the Christians and destroy them. Yuval wrote on the role that yearning for the elimination of the Christians plays in the Jewish dream of messianic redemption. He emphasized that the prayer does not ask God to help the Jews murder the Christians—vengeance is to be carried out by heaven. Yuval found this approach principally among Ashkenazic Jews. Sephardis, he wrote, tended more to pray for the Christians to convert to Judaism upon the arrival of the Messiah. Yuval found similarities between Christian hatred of Jews and Jewish hatred of Christians. Jews burned effigies of Haman, the villain of the Book of Esther; Christians burned Jews themselves. Yuval tried to understand them both.

The article sparked a scandal. Yuval was accused of attempting to justify the murder of Jews in the medieval period, as if they were guilty of what was done to them. His article turned the victim into a murderer, his critics charged. Yuval's response: "Such shocking words are unprecedented in Jewish studies polemics." As the debate progressed, it also addressed the question of whether a Jewish historian should publish research findings that are liable to hurt Jews. Said

Yuval, "Are we, because of the fabrications of antisemites, to turn the study of our history into a propaganda poster?"

Echoes of the debate sounded beyond the narrow bounds of the academy, but for the most part it remained within *Zion*, a fairly obscure periodical. In contrast, an article by Ze'ev Herzog, a Tel Aviv University professor of archaeology, set off a truly public storm. It appeared at the end of 1999, again, in *Ha'aretz*'s weekend magazine. He brought the argument to a new level, even more threatening than the polemic over Zionism itself.

Herzog wrote that seventy years of energetic excavation had failed to turn up any archaeological proof of many of the foundation stories of the Bible, the Jewish "title deed" to its land: "The Israelites were never in Egypt, did not wander in the desert, did not conquer the land in a military campaign, and did not pass it on to the twelve tribes of Israel. Furthermore, the united monarchy of David and Solomon, which is described by the Bible as a regional power, was at most a small tribal kingdom."

The claim is not new. German scholars in the nineteenth century had argued that the history of Israel as related in the Bible was in fact a much later invention. Archaeology sought, however, to prove that the Bible was correct. This was the goal of the non-Jewish archaeologists who excavated in Palestine before the establishment of the state, William Albright foremost among them. It was also the position of the first generation of Israeli archaeologists, whose leading figure was Yigael Yadin. "Slowly, cracks began to appear in the picture," Herzog

wrote. "Paradoxically . . . the glut of findings began to undermine the historical credibility of the biblical descriptions
instead of reinforcing them." He gave a list of examples:

The patriarchal period. Scholars had a hard time agreeing on
which archaeological period matched the time of the patriarchs. When did Abraham, Isaac, and Jacob live? When was
their tomb, the Machpela Cave in Hebron, purchased?

*The Exodus from Egypt, the wandering in the desert, and Mount
Sinai.* The many Egyptian documents known to us do not mention the Israelite sojourn in Egypt or the Exodus. Generations
of scholars have tried to locate Mount Sinai and the stations
the Israelite tribes passed through in the desert. Intensive
research has failed to find even one site that matches the biblical portrayal of these events. Most historians today agree that,
at best, the sojourn in Egypt and the Exodus were the experiences of a few families whose private story was expanded and
"nationalized" for ideological or theological purposes.

The conquest of the Land of Israel. As more and more sites
were uncovered in Palestine, it turned out that Canaanite
cities had been destroyed or abandoned at different times, and
not in the face of one concerted onslaught. This seemed to
indicate that there was no basis for the biblical story of the
conquest of the land by the Israelite tribes under the leadership
of Joshua.

Many of these findings, Herzog wrote, had been known
to scholars for some time but they had not made their way
into the public consciousness. Herzog offered a political
explanation:

Biblical historiography was one of the foundation stones in the construction of Israeli Jewish society's national identity. The secular population in Israel, which rejected the legal-religious foundations of the Talmud, took the Bible to its heart. Biblical historiography expressed in the Torah and in the books of Joshua, Judges, Kings, and Chronicles, which were composed as ideological and theological works, has become the foundation of Israeli secular culture. The close link to the land and its landscape has been channeled into archaeology, which has become a national hobby of unearthing the Jewish people's forefathers and kings. . . .

Challenging the reliability of the biblical accounts is seen as a challenge to "our historic right to the land" and as shattering the myth of the nation reestablishing the ancient Israeli kingdom. These symbolic elements are such an important component of Israeli identity that every attempt to ponder their truth runs into antagonism or avoidance. . . .

It turns out that part of Israeli society is ready to recognize the injustice that was done to Arab inhabitants of the country and is willing to accept the principle of equal rights for women—but is not sturdy enough to adopt the archaeological facts that shatter the biblical myth."

Herzog's article prompted a deluge of responses, some sympathetic, and a large number of discussions in which thousands of people participated. Herzog was right about the debate's political dimension. A letter to the participants in one of the seminars on the issue stated: "We live in a turbulent era of an existential struggle for the Land of Israel. The peace talks with the Palestinians are extremely risky. And here the recent archaeological polemic includes approaches that border on those of Palestinian propagandists who claim that Arab identity has roots in the Canaanite nation, and that the primal right to the land thus belongs not to the Hebrew patriarchs but to ancient Arab tribes." The letter concludes: "Our time is caught up in an earthshaking issue: a struggle for peace and for the land in which we live. It now looks as if we must also defend our national spiritual asset—the Bible. Our national identity is based on the heritage of generations sustained by it."

Against this background, and in the wake of the Rabin assassination, a reexamination began of Jewish-Arab relations within Israel. Journalist Salman Masalha wrote: "The Rabin assassination was an attempt to murder Israel's growing normalcy when it was still in its infancy. He was killed to preserve the Jewish family's honor. That's one of the reasons for the cheers heard from a small section of the Jewish community here and overseas. I predict that the next struggle will not be over the question of who is a Jew. It will be over who is an Israeli. In that war, all citizens, Jews and Arabs, will be partners."

The struggle took place, in part, in the Knesset.

• • •

Minister of Education Yossi Sarid, leader of the left-wing Meretz party, announced at the end of February 2000 that some poems by Mahmoud Darwish would henceforth be included in the list of literature teachers could choose for their classes. Darwish, an exiled Israeli Arab who became a leader of the PLO, is considered one of the greatest modern Arab poets. Sanctioning his poems in the classroom set off a controversy. Prime Minister Ehud Barak said that the innovation had come too early. The subject was brought up for discussion on several occasions in the Knesset, once in the context of a no-confidence motion. The transcripts of these debates reveal the depths of the Israeli pressure cooker, in which memory and anxiety float to the surface alternatively, as do hope, despair, fear, hatred, politics, poetics and demagogy, God and love of one's fellow man, Zionism and the Holocaust, discrimination, terrorism, morality, and national honor. Only a very fractured and confused society could produce such exchanges, and they are well worth reading. Here are some selections.

Uzi Landau (Likud, right-wing): "The school system thinks that values and principles don't matter. In the State of Israel . . . populism dictates the national agenda. . . . This education system is teaching children to doubt the justice of Zionism's achievements. It is cutting away at the Jewish and Zionist roots of our culture. It is a system that produces ignorance and derision of our heritage. . . .

"When they say more Darwish there's less Bialik. There is less Zionism and more post-Zionism and less Jewish history and more fabricated Palestinian history and fabricated Zionist and Jewish history. . . . We are in the throes of the de-Zionization of Israel. . . . I'm sorry that even the prime minister has in recent months been saying 'Israel is the country of all its citizens.' Not a Jewish state, not a Zionist state, but a state of all its citizens. That's the emphasis. And here we are on that slippery slope.

"Mahmoud Darwish is a case in point. He's presented as the greatest Palestinian poet of his generation. I'm not acquainted with his poetry. . . . But he negates our existence, he despises us, he loathes us, he wants our destruction, as he writes: 'The time has come for you to get out / for you to die wherever you want / take your dead and leave / our continent, our sea.' And Minister Sarid says: 'This is literature. . . . We should study it to become acquainted with the enemy, with the Palestinians, through literature. . . .'"

Uzi Landau went on to say that the school system had failed. "Under the great slogans of liberalism, humanism, and democracy it is jettisoning the State of Israel's Jewish content, which children should be exposed to from a young age. . . . When principles are drained out of education, the result is political and military weakness, broken will, weariness. We don't stand up for what is ours and we don't speak honestly about ourselves; in recent years we've given in on almost everything . . ."

Yossi Sarid: "The new literature curriculum is immeasurably superior to its predecessor, which was prepared 21 years ago. It includes the classics, but also modern writers. It is more open and more sensitive to Israel's multicultural character. For the first time it is mandatory—take note, mandatory—to teach not only Bialik, Agnon, and the poets of the Golden Age of Spain, but also [classic Zionist poets such as] Shaul Tchernikhovsky, Uri Zvi Greenberg, Natan Alterman, Rahel, Leah Goldberg [and acclaimed modern poets] Yehuda Amichai and Natan Zach. It is a curriculum worthy of the name, even an appropriately Zionist curriculum. These are required poets.

"In my opinion it's also important to open a window onto the culture of our Arab neighbors and Israel's Arab citizens. It's not good to be closed off; it's not good to live in a cultural ghetto. It is good to learn, to get to know things. To study doesn't mean to identify. I, for example, do not identify in any way with the poetry of Uri Zvi Greenberg [a right-wing nationalist poet], which often offends me and about which I have many reservations. . . . He has written a few terrible, horrible, unacceptable and unworthy poems about the kibbutz movement, about Mishmar Haemek: 'May you have no children, may you have no rain.' It's a dreadful curse, but during my tenure, not someone else's, he is part of the curriculum, a required poet, not shut out."

Roni Milo (Center Party): "My fear, my problem, is not Darwish. My fear is that they're not studying enough Israeli history, that they're not studying enough about the land of Israel, that they're not studying enough history of the Jewish people. That's my fear. If they have that, I'm not scared of Darwish."

Meir Porush (Agudat Yisrael): "The day is not far off when the minister of education will decide that we won't read the

Book of Esther on Purim, because he does not like it, but rather the poems of Mahmoud Darwish."

Michael Kleiner (Likud, right wing): "The larger, ultimate plan of the education minister is to establish a mixed Jewish-Arab school system where children will learn to know one another firsthand, will learn to stop hating, will learn to love, will learn to fall in love, perhaps, and get married, perhaps to bring children into the world, and in the heat of their love end the Jewish-Arab conflict. . . . Yossi Sarid is a racist clothed in enlightenment. He doesn't act like someone who wants a Jewish state. He is prepared to accept any other state, just not a Jewish one. If that's not racism, what is?"

Re'uven Rivlin (Likud): "I understand we are a nation that has to a large extent lost its need for symbols, for an ethos, for a tradition that has led us and brought us to this point, but still there is a matter of honor . . . There's no censorship. You can buy Darwish in every store. He's translated [into Hebrew] and whoever wants to can pick up his books. But to put him onto the school agenda—that makes a statement: that says there's no honor, you can do whatever you want with us, because we aren't worth anything."

Nissim Ze'ev (Shas): "Yossi Sarid teaches self-hatred and is considered an enemy of Jewish culture."

Sarid: "What insults me as an Israeli, a Jew and, I would say, as a Zionist is the great panic that has come over the Knesset and certain political circles . . . as if the greatest strategic threat to Israel today is Mahmoud Darwish's poetry. This is absolutely shameful. Why all this fear and trembling? Why are you so scared of Darwish? . . . Why this hysteria? You are all fine, upstanding patriots, full of confidence. But we [on the left] have much more self-confidence and self-respect. We have much more faith in our students."

The no-confidence motion over the inclusion of Mahmoud Darwish's poems in the school curriculum was narrowly defeated, 47 to 42.

The post-Zionist challenge is to create arrangements that will allow Israelis of all kinds to live together, in keeping with the two greatest influences on the country: America and Judaism. The public discourse on this is still at its very beginnings. At this point, the debate is largely over the question of how Israel can be both a Jewish and a democratic state.

In recent years, the tension between Israel's Jewish character and democratic nature has preoccupied many thinkers and writers and has produced a series of books. As the debate grew more intense, Ruth Gavison, a professor of law and an expert on civil rights, reached the conclusion that it was neither impossible nor unjust to combine the state's Jewish character with the principles of democracy. The assumption is that Israel will remain a Jewish state as long as a majority of its citizens define themselves as Jews and want there to be such a state.

Gavison likened the status of Israel's Arab citizens to the status of the Jews in the United States. Most Americans are

Christians. "Christianity is part of most Americans' self-description," Gavison wrote, "and also part of the country's self-description, despite the official separation of church and state. There can be no doubt that Jews who maintain an active connection to their Judaism feel, in this situation, a certain sense of alienation, of not completely belonging. Problems of belonging and of identity exist in every state and should be attended to. Nevertheless, the fact that an identity problem exists does not make a country undemocratic." The Arab citizens of Israel, Gavison wrote, enjoy significant and equal political rights and no small measure of personal freedom and security. She does not believe that their sense of alienation justifies the assertion that Israel is not a democratic state.

Gavison maintains that the Zionist enterprise can be justified morally, but tends to concentrate on the concrete questions that arise from Israel being a Jewish state: "The practical question is not whether the Jews had the right to establish a demographic-territorial concentration in Palestine, but what is the justifiable cost that can be demanded from other groups—largely the country's Arab inhabitants—for the realization of the existing Jewish community's right to live under conditions of self-determination and security." The question that engages Gavison is whether the damage suffered by the country's Arab inhabitants is so high as to "take precedence over the right of the Jewish people to a state in which it governs and in which it is the majority." In her opinion, the maintenance of the Jewish national state is justified. Gavison does not, however, justify Israeli rule over the territories; she calls for the establishment of a Palestinian state. Having determined that Israel is a Jewish, democratic state, Gavison analyzes a series of actions aimed at increasing equality between Jews and Arabs and encouraging Arab integration into public life.

Sami Smooha, a professor of sociology at the University of Haifa, has called for cultural autonomy for Israel's Arabs. The plan would not provide territorial autonomy but rather the right of the entire Arab community to administer a number of matters itself. The idea would have been heresy just a few years ago, yet it does not necessarily reflect post-Zionist ideological tendencies. Instead, it results from new circumstances in which Israel's Arabs live.

When riots broke out in the territories at the end of 2000 the Arabs of Israel were also stirred up. Police brutality amplified the Arabs' anger and made their alienation all the more profound. Nonetheless, the circumstances of their lives are very different from those of the Palestinians in the territories. More involved in the country's life than in the past, aware of their rights as citizens, and enjoying a greater measure of civil equality, the Arabs in Israel are all the more aware of their double identities as Israelis of Palestinian nationality and have searched for appropriate ways to express this.

Smooha's guiding assumptions are that the Israeli Arab community is developing as a separate entity that has its own agenda and interests, and that Israel's definition as a Jewish state contradicts full equality for its Arab citizens. Israel denies the existence of a common civil nation; according to its fundamental philosophy, the state belongs to the Jewish people, which means not to all its citizens. The Basic Law: Human Dignity and Liberty is supposed to guarantee democratic rights for all its citizens, including its Arab citizens, but it also defines Israel as Jewish and democratic. The law governing political parties does not allow a group to stand for election if it denies the definition of Israel as the state of the Jewish people. Hebrew is the dominant language; Arabic, while an official language, has an inferior status. The country's name and the governing calendar are Hebrew. The national anthem, flag, memorial days, historic sites, heroes, and other symbols are exclusively Jewish.

The state is considered the direct successor of the Jewish sovereign entity that ended with the destruction of the Second Temple two thousand years ago. The Holocaust is a central component of Israeli identity. The Law of Return grants the right to immigrate to Israel and receive immediate citizenship exclusively to Jews and their relatives, while few people enter the country under the immigration law that applies to non-Jews. The state encourages the immigration of Jews and grants them an aid package. The state gives preference to its Jewish citizens in distributing government grants to municipalities, development projects, and capital investments and also gives them preference with regard to taxation and services. Arab citizens find it very difficult to secure work in government and public institutions, including the universities. The Jewish

Agency and the Jewish National Fund carry out manifestly governmental functions such as the planning of new settlements and their support, forestation, the preservation and lease of land, the maintenance of welfare institutions, and the funding of cultural activities.

Smooha has pointed out that most Israeli Arabs live apart from the country's Jews, despite the increasing number who have moved to mixed cities. As an ethnic democracy—that is, both Jewish and democratic—Smooha has written, Israel cannot solve the problem of its Arab minority by granting full equality and integration. It must take advantage of the existing separation to establish nonterritorial autonomy for its Arab citizens.

According to Smooha, in its full, institutionalized form, establishing autonomy would require a referendum of the Arabs listed in the election rolls. After approval, the Knesset would pass a law empowering a supreme Arab council with an executive committee. This committee would be authorized to represent the Arab population to the authorities in all areas of public life, including policy, budgets, and communications. A mediation mechanism would be set up to resolve disputes. The autonomous authority would be allowed to appoint representatives in Israeli embassies and sign agreements with other countries and non-Israeli bodies, including Palestine and the Arab countries, with the approval of the Israeli government. There would be equality of all the country's citizens and mandatory national service for all. Each citizen would be given a choice between military and civilian service.

The autonomous authority and its institutions would have a language, a symbol, a flag, an anthem, a calendar, memorial days, sites, and other symbols of their own, so long as they did not contradict Israeli law.

Smooha believes autonomy could be instituted gradually. At the first stage the state would not even have to recognize the Arabs as a national minority and would not have to set up elected institutions for them. It would be sufficient, he maintains, to establish equivalence between the Arab and ultra-Orthodox populations. The Arabs would receive control of the school system, radio and television broadcasts, the Muslim and Christian departments in the Ministry of Religious Affairs, and the Muslim Waqf (the body that controls Muslim religious properties). They would be allowed to establish Arabic-language institutions of higher education, including a university, which would enjoy academic freedom and receive the same funding granted to other Israeli academic institutions. The Knesset would revise the country's laws to ensure that Arabs receive appropriate representation in government, public authorities, and state corporations. It would become accepted practice for Arab parties to join governing coalitions and be appointed cabinet ministers, Supreme Court justices, and directors-general of government ministries.

Israeli Jews of all persuasions, including those on the liberal left, cannot accept Smooha's proposals because they violate their most fundamental conception of the country. The proposals cannot even be reconciled with those post-Zionist views that advocate the revocation of the country's Jewish-Zionist character and its transformation into a liberal, multinational democracy. Smooha is not optimistic. It would seem that only the Arabs themselves could promote such an arrangement— and that would require an energetic, long-term struggle, including one within the Arab community. Not all Israeli Arabs support the idea, partly out of fear that such "autonomy" would make their inferior civil status permanent. Even the idea's supporters disagree on the details.

Conclusion

Just a few minutes after Likud parliamentarian Moshe Katzav was elected Israel's eighth president, Limor Livnat, a Knesset member from the same party, who would soon become minister of education in Ariel Sharon's government, described his success as the victory of Zionism over post-Zionism. The truth is that Katzav's margin of victory had come from Shas, the non-Zionist, ultra-Orthodox party. Shimon Peres, the losing candidate, is one of the state's founding fathers. Livnat's declaration demonstrated the right's tendency to monopolize Zionism; once the left had done the same.

Either way, Katzav's biography is very Israeli. His is an American-style success story. Born in Iran, he came to Israel as a boy, grew up in immigrant transit camps, and raised himself to the country's highest office. Conclusion: every boy can grow up to be president. Just like in America. Katzav is a religious man, and his spoken Hebrew betrays his country of origin. He is a very Jewish Israeli.

The country he serves as president differs greatly from the one he found when he came as a child. Never has Israel been farther from the vision of David Ben-Gurion, yet in the past fifty years, the Zionist movement has come close to realizing all its goals. Soon, for the first time in two millennia, the largest Jewish community in the world will be in Israel. Most of the Jews who want to settle in the country will have done so by then; henceforth, the "ingathering of the Exiles" will be but a thin stream of immigrants. The Law of Return will, for all intents and purposes, have lost its meaning. Presumably the number of Jews in the world will decline, largely as a result of intermarriage. The relative proportion of ultra-Orthodox non-Zionists among those remaining will grow. When that happens, Israel will have entered the age of post-Zionism. Zionism, if at all relevant, may no longer be useful for describing the nature of the relations between Israel and the Jewish world. At most, it would define relations between Israelis and Arabs and among Israelis themselves.

But then, at the end of 1999, as more and more Israelis seemed to be adopting post-Zionist concepts, a new *intifada* broke out and the Oslo process fell apart. On the right, no one was surprised. "We told you there was no one to talk to," they said. On the left, some people were taken aback, while some were insulted. "How could you do this to us?" they said to their Palestinian friends. "Now, of all times, when we're ready to talk about partitioning Jerusalem." As elections for prime minister approached in 2001, Israelis began to think that there was no solution to the conflict, at least not in their generation. Perhaps it is possible to manage the conflict through partial arrangements, but it is apparently impossible to resolve.

In the creeping post-Zionist atmosphere of a certain indifference toward politics and ideology, there was a strange, even forced, aspect to the renewed confrontation with existential questions—questions that for many had seemed part of the past. The most pressing of these was the right of return for Palestinian refugees who had either fled or been driven out of the country in 1948. A group of Israeli peace activists, among them the novelists Amos Oz and A. B. Yehoshua, published a full-page advertisement in *Ha'aretz* rejecting the refugees' right of return: "We recognize the urgent and real need to solve the problem of the 1948 refugees," they wrote. "We also recognize the State of Israel's partial responsibility for creating the problem. These refugees will have the right to return to their homeland, Palestine, and settle there. But we wish to make clear that we cannot agree to the refugees' return to the territory that is part of the State of Israel, because that is tantamount to Israel's destruction. There can certainly be humanitarian solutions regarding the unification of individual families, but an across-the-board return of Palestinian refugees to Israel contradicts the principle of the right of self-determination for the Jewish people. Alongside the right of self-determination for Palestinians, this principle constitutes the moral basis for the agreement that will be signed between the two peoples."

In the twenty years prior to the Oslo agreement, several of Israel's inviolable "thou shalt nots" were broken, including the prohibitions against negotiating with the PLO, giving up territories without peace, agreeing to a Palestinian state, and in the end discussing the division of Jerusalem. The willingness of the advertisement's signatories to recognize Israel's partial responsibility for the Palestinian tragedy broke another taboo. So it is not totally outside the realm of possibility that Israel will someday also recognize the refugees' right of return. However, at the time, the refusal to recognize Palestinian right of return was a matter of very broad Israeli consensus.

Then Ariel Sharon became prime minister. Ehud Barak was not ousted for betraying the nation's sacred values but mostly because he failed to reach an agreement with the Palestinians. Shas's voters punished him because of the attempt during his tenure to interfere with their school system and impose a foreign secular worldview. Arab voters boycotted the elections to protest the deaths of thirteen Arab-Israeli demonstrators shot by police during disturbances at the outbreak of the new *intifada*.

In his seventies, Sharon comes from the country's founding generation. He is a mythological figure, larger than life, and represents the spirit of the 1950s. Fittingly, he described the new *intifada* as another round of Israel's War of Independence; Israelis have responded by falling back into the tribal siege mentality that marked the state's early days and calling for unity, along the lines of the original Zionist struggle. The minister of education has begun to phase out the new history textbooks, replacing them with older, more "Zionist" ones. Commentators have reverted to condemning criticism from the outside world, particulary from Europe, as anti-Israeli, even as disguised anti-Semitism. Israelis voice fewer objections to violations of Palestinian human rights, including torture. As bombs continue to explode in towns all over Israel, walls in downtown Jerusalem have been covered with graffiti that proclaims, "No Arabs—No Terror." Once again, it has become acceptable to hate Arabs openly.

At times, history seems to have turned backward. A comment made by British major general Bernard Montgomery comes to mind: "The Jew murders the Arab and the Arab murders the Jew. This is what is going on in Palestine now, and it will go on for the next fifty years in all probability." Unlike the British, however, Israelis and Palestinians have nowhere to go. Meanwhile, Palestinian terror has pushed Israel back into the Zionist womb; this may be the Palestinians' idea of revenge. Hence post-Zionism is out at present. But the deeper developments that indicated a post-Zionist future were evidence of something Israelis had begun to recognize: There is life after Zionism.

Notes

Introduction

5   When peace comes: A.B. Yehoshua, *In the Name of Normalcy* (Tel Aviv: Schocken, 1980), p. 139.

Facing Herzl's Statue

28   If the Arabs imagine: Joseph Klausner, "After the Disturbances," *Ha'aretz*, 3 April 1920, p. 3.

Facing Elvis's Statue

61   I view the tightening: Yitzhak Rabin, *Pinkas Sherut* (Tel Aviv: Sifriat Ma'ariv, 1979), vol I, p. 213.

67   It began on: Sami Shalom Shitrit, *The Ashkenazi Revolution is Over: Comments on Israel From a Dark Perspective* (Tel Aviv: Bimat Kedem Lesifrut, 1999), pp. 107.

69   These kids have: Ibid. p. 110.

Facing Ovadia's Statue

89   The important and: Uriel Simon, "Secular-Religious Cooperation in Building a Democratic Jewish State," *Alpai'im*, 1996, vol. 13, p. 154.

91   There is one general: Tzvi Yehuda Kook, quoted in Yigal Eilam, *Ketz hayahadut—umat hadat ve'hamamlacha* (Tel Aviv: Am Oved, 2000), p. 274.

96   I met happy: David Ohana, *Humanist in the Sun: Camus and Mediterranean Inspiration* (Jerusalem: Magnes Press, 2000), p. 122.

109   When the founders: Gershom Schocken, "Ezra's Curse," *Ha'aretz*, 29 August 1985.

110   The centrality of: Hanoch Marmari, "The Law of Return," *Ha'aretz*, 11 November 1994.

Facing Gadi Manella's Statue:

117   Two shots: Eli Amir, "Exile at Home," from *Yitzhak Rabin, 1922–1952* (Tel Aviv: Sifriat Ma'ariv, 1998), p. 149.

133   Post-Zionism was: Yoram Hazony, *The Jewish State: The Struggle for Israel's Soul* (New York: Basic Books, 2000), pp. xxvi–vii.

135   an anti-Zionist propaganda: Akiva Eldar, "The Education of Lies: Who Took Control of the History Books," *Ha'aretz*, 24 August 2000.

136   The message is: Aharon Megged, "The Israeli Urge to Suicide," *Ha'aretz*, 10 June 1994.

139   Post-Zionist ideology: Eliezer Schweid, *The Zionism After Zionism*, (Jerusalem: WZO, 1997), p. 7.

140   We will continue: Ilan Pappe, "A Lesson in New History," *Ha'aretz*, 24 June 1994.

142   Slowly, cracks began: Ze'ev Herzog, *Ha'aretz*, weekend magazine, 12 December 1999.

Index

Index

About the Author

Tom Segev is a columnist for *Ha'aretz*, Israel's leading newspaper. He is author of three now-classic works on the history of Israel, among them *One Palestine, Complete: Jews and Arabs Under the British Mandate*, which received the National Jewish Book Award and was a *New York Times* Editors' Choice of 2000. He lives in Jerusalem.